The **Essential Guide** to **Driving in Europe**

Europe

Drive safely
and stay legal in

50

countries!

VELOCE PUBLISHING
THE PUBLISHER OF FINE AUTOMOTIVE BOOKS

Julian Parish

For post publication news, updates and amendments relating to this book visit:
www.veloce.co.uk/books/V4788

www.veloce.co.uk

First published March 2016 by Veloce Publishing Limited, Veloce House, Parkway Farm Business Park, Middle Farm Way, Poundbury, Dorchester DT1 3AR, England.
Fax 01305 268864 / e-mail info@veloce.co.uk / web www.veloce.co.uk or www.velocebooks.com.
ISBN: 978-1-845847-88-3 UPC: 6-36847-04788-7 © 2016 Julian Parish and Veloce Publishing. All rights reserved. With the exception of quoting brief passages for the purpose of review, no part of this publication may be recorded, reproduced or transmitted by any means, including photocopying, without the written permission of Veloce Publishing Ltd. Throughout this book logos, model names and designations, etc, have been used for the purposes of identification, illustration and decoration. Such names are the property of the trademark holder as this is not an official publication. Readers with ideas for automotive books, or books on other transport or related hobby subjects, are invited to write to the editorial director of Veloce Publishing at the above address. British Library Cataloguing in Publication Data – A catalogue record for this book is available from the British Library. Typesetting, design and page make-up all by Veloce Publishing Ltd. Printed in India by Replika Press.

Contents

i *Cover photo: the A41 autoroute from Annecy to Geneva. (Courtesy APRR/Véronique Paul)*

Introduction

When the car rental firm Avis set out recently to find the world's best driving roads, 18 of its top 25 were in Europe. Whether you're a diehard motoring enthusiast, or looking forward to a family holiday by car, Europe has some great roads to explore.

Over the past 30 years, I have driven more than half a million miles across Europe, for business and on holiday, in my own or hire cars, and few things can beat the freedom and enjoyment of travelling by road. Modern cars are generally more reliable and better suited to long journeys than ever before. Despite some recent increases, accident rates have come down over the past decade, and road conditions have greatly improved.

For many travellers though, driving in a foreign country can still be a worrisome process, especially the first time. Very few motorists will have the misfortune to be involved in an accident, but breakdowns and inadvertent parking tickets can beset us all. Driving styles abroad can be very different from what you are used to, and newspapers regularly run features with headlines like "Bonkers Belgians, perilous Poles ..." (*The Sunday Times*). A little preparation can do much to help your trip go smoothly, which is where this guide comes in.

In the sections for each country, you'll find information on the most important regulations for car drivers, clearly and consistently presented. It's easy to cover ground quickly in Europe, and border crossings soon come round: despite increasing EU harmonisation, there are still many differences between neighbouring countries. Every effort has been made to check that this information is correct and up-to-date, but changes will occur. You should always pay attention to local signs or directions from police officers. Surprisingly, supposedly official sources often give contradictory information; in case of doubt, I have always taken the most conservative approach.

Inevitably, a book like this is full of rules and warnings, and I hope you will never need to put some of the information here to the test. Instead, I hope you will get as much pleasure from your trips as I have done from mine.

Enjoy your travels!

Julian Parish
Paris, France

Using the guide

This guide provides plenty of signposts
to help keep you safe and within the law
on your drives through Europe.

This guide is divided into five chapters, helping you to easily find the information you need (❶). Chapter 1, *Driving in a foreign country* (❷), provides general advice, regardless of the country you are visiting. You'll find lots of information on dealing with different driving conditions, with convenient sections covering everything from winter driving, to what to do in an emergency.

Chapters 2-5 contain essential information for 50 countries, grouped into four regions: *Western Europe*, *Southern Europe*, *Northern Europe*, and *Central & Eastern Europe*. The sections for each country include what to watch out for, illustrations of road signs (❸), and the key information needed to stay safe and legal.

Chapters

Driving in a foreign country ❷
Western Europe ❸
Southern Europe ❸
Northern Europe ❸
Central & Eastern Europe ❸

Each of the main chapters carry a colour-coded top bar.

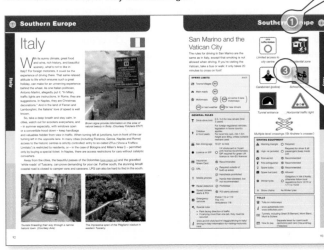

Road signs

Many entries in this guide include descriptions of road and traffic signs, many of which are likely to be unfamiliar.

Driving abroad

Chapter 1 is full of general advice on driving abroad.

What, where and how fast ...

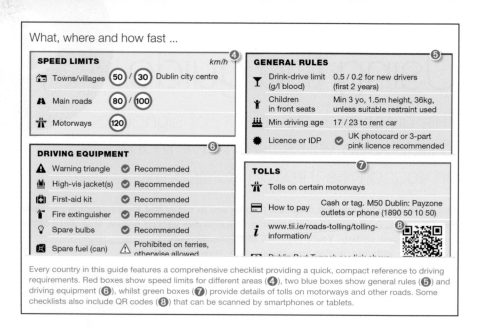

SPEED LIMITS *km/h* ④

🏠 Towns/villages	(50) / (30)	Dublin city centre
🛣 Main roads	(80) / (100)	
🛫 Motorways	(120)	

GENERAL RULES ⑤

🍷	Drink-drive limit (g/l blood)	0.5 / 0.2 for new drivers (first 2 years)
👶	Children in front seats	Min 3 yo, 1.5m height, 36kg, unless suitable restraint used
👥	Min driving age	17 / 23 to rent car
✴	Licence or IDP	● UK photocard or 3-part pink licence recommended

DRIVING EQUIPMENT ⑥

⚠ Warning triangle	●	Recommended
🦺 High-vis jacket(s)	●	Recommended
🧰 First-aid kit	●	Recommended
🧯 Fire extinguisher	●	Recommended
💡 Spare bulbs	●	Recommended
⛽ Spare fuel (can)	⚠	Prohibited on ferries, otherwise allowed

TOLLS ⑦

🛫	Tolls on certain motorways	
💳	How to pay	Cash or tag. M50 Dublin: Payzone outlets or phone (1890 50 10 50)
i	www.tii.ie/roads-tolling/tolling-information/	⑧

Every country in this guide features a comprehensive checklist providing a quick, compact reference to driving requirements. Red boxes show speed limits for different areas (④), two blue boxes show general rules (⑤) and driving equipment (⑥), whilst green boxes (⑦) provide details of tolls on motorways and other roads. Some checklists also include QR codes (⑧) that can be scanned by smartphones or tablets.

Handy checklists cover speed limits (④), general rules (⑤), the driving equipment you'll need (⑥), and motorway tolls (⑦).

For countries with cross-Channel ports, an extra section provides information on crossings, with contact details for ferry operators, and a map of the port (⑨). In the Alps, each country has a special feature covering the major mountain passes and tunnels, with details of the maximum gradient, opening times, and tolls (⑩).

Throughout the guide, you'll find URLs and – for smartphone users – QR codes, taking you to websites with further information (⑧). At the end of the guide, links to additional online services provide continuously updated details of fuel prices, traffic conditions and more.

Port information

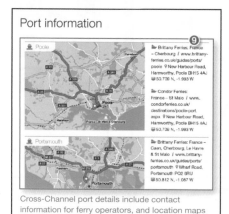

Cross-Channel port details include contact information for ferry operators, and location maps with GPS coordinates, as well as overview maps showing the major routes away from the ports.

Mountain passes and tunnels

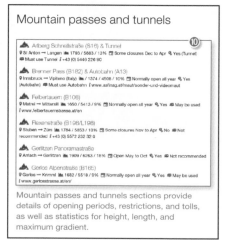

Mountain passes and tunnels sections provide details of opening periods, restrictions, and tolls, as well as statistics for height, length, and maximum gradient.

Europe & the EU

From tiny San Marino, to the vast expanse of Russia, Europe's diverse countries draw millions of visitors each year.

Encompassing the frozen Arctic Circle in the north, and the heat of the Mediterranean in the south, the range and variety of its landscapes, cultures and history ensures that there's always somewhere new to explore.

Not to be confused with the continent of Europe, the European Union (EU) is a socio-economic group that comprises 28 countries – known as 'member states' – from across the region (see page 50). The map below shows the countries covered in this guide, with member states shown in **blue**, and non-member states shown in **dark green**.

Note: Every effort has been made to check all the information in this guide carefully, but changes will inevitably occur, for which the author and publisher cannot be held responsible. **Please check with the national authorities before traveling, especially if you are driving a minibus or motor caravan, or towing a trailer, and to check current prices.**

Thank you!

A huge number of organisations and individuals provided help and information during the preparation of this guide. Photos are credited throughout the text, but I would particularly like to thank the national tourist boards and other government agencies in each country, as well as several European-wide organisations, which include: AIT/FIA Information Centre, the European Commission, ETSC (European Transport Safety Council), TISPOL (European Traffic Police Network), YOURS (Youth for Road Safety), and the website DriveEuropeNews.com.

A great deal of information – much of it not published in English – has been supplied by European motoring associations, among them the ÖAMTC (Austria), Touring Belgium, Bison Futé and Prévention Routière (France), ADAC (Germany), ACI (Italy) and TCS (Switzerland), as well as the AA, Caravan Club and RAC (United Kingdom).

Many other organisations helped the author. They include Eurotunnel and the cross-Channel ferry companies, port authorities in the UK and on the Continent, motorway operators in France (Autoroutes de France) and Portugal (Via Verde), car hire firms such as Avis and Sixt, and suppliers of touring equipment, including John Jordan Limited, Ring Automotive, and TomTom.

None of this information would be in your hands now without the hard work of the tremendous team at Veloce Publishing, and especially Rod Grainger, Kevin Atkins, Joe Russell and Paul Castle. Jude Brooks, publisher of Veloce's sister imprint, Hubble & Hattie, provided expert advice for the section on travelling with pets. Finally, I would like to thank all the friends who supported and encouraged me as I worked on this book, and in particular Nic and Joc Ridley, and Marie Augereau.

Julian Parish

Driving in a foreign country

Driving towards Öræfajökull, Iceland's highest peak.
(Courtesy Visit Iceland)

1

The first time

Whether you're an exchange student or newly retired, there's a first time for everyone driving abroad.

If you're already an experienced driver in your home country, there's no reason why driving in another country should be especially daunting. The first couple of days will seem strange, though, so don't overdo things: tackling rush hour traffic in a busy foreign capital on your first day probably isn't a good idea!

Don't let these unfamiliar signs put you off! (Courtesy ÖAMTC)

Taking your own car abroad has the advantage that it will already be familiar to you, and some local drivers will be more considerate to strangers in their area. On the downside, you may have a long drive to reach your final destination, and in some countries the steering wheel will be on the 'wrong' side of the car (see page 26 for advice on coping with this).

Crossing the Channel: boarding Le Shuttle. (Courtesy Eurotunnel)

If you're picking up a hire car in a country where they drive on the other side of the road to your home country, it will initially seem odd, including changing gear with the 'wrong' hand, but you'll be on the correct side of the car for better visibility. When you rent a car in a foreign country, however, there are a few extra things to think about:

Collecting the keys. (Courtesy TCS)

- Since 2015 it has been necessary to provide **evidence of your driving record**: UK drivers, for example, can call the DVLA or obtain a code to access it online at www.gov.uk/view-driving-licence
- Even if you plan on doing all the driving, **ask one of your passengers to bring their licence** in case of emergencies, and have the rental company add them to the agreement
- Check the **age limits for hiring a car** with the different rental companies: some apply restrictions for drivers under 23 or over 70
- If you expect to **cross into another country or use gravel roads** (eg, in Tuscany), make sure this is covered
- Check the **insurance** included in the hire agreement, and consider paying the additional premium for improved accident cover
- Don't hesitate to ask rental company staff to explain the **car's controls and safety equipment** to you. It might be the first time, for example, that you have driven a car with an electronic handbrake
- Check that all the **safety equipment required locally** – from reflective jackets to winter tyres – is present. See the checklists in chapters 2-5 for more details

It's all worthwhile: enjoying the view beside a brand-new Mercedes camper. (Courtesy Daimler AG)

The first time

Preparing your car

Long distances, extra loads, extreme heat or cold; steep gradients, rough roads ... a little advance planning will ensure that your car copes safely with your trip to another country.

Before you go, get your car serviced, especially if you typically use it for short journeys, or if it's older and no longer under warranty. Get the air-conditioning checked, and make sure the brakes and tyres are in good condition. You may need to increase the tyre pressures for heavy loads or sustained high speed cruising, especially in Germany.

Set tyre pressures correctly. (Courtesy ADAC)

In some areas of Europe, only lower grade petrol (95 or even 92 octane) will be available, and your car's engine may need adjustment. If your car doesn't have one already, fitting a passenger door mirror will make changing lanes easier.

Everyone's nightmare: a winter breakdown. (Courtesy ÖAMTC)

If you're driving on the opposite side of the road to home, you'll need to adjust your headlamps to avoid dazzling oncoming traffic: some cars have levers or controls you can adjust yourself, but xenon headlamps on newer cars may need to be re-set by your dealer. Otherwise, it's a legal requirement in most countries to use stick-on headlamp beam converters. Remember, too, to adjust the headlamp beam height if your car will be heavily loaded. You may be able to change the speedometer settings to display kilometres per hour (km/h) or miles per hour (mph), which may make it easier to keep to speed limits.

Finally, don't forget a sticker, showing the country where your car is registered, for the back of your car, or – for most EU countries – a rear number plate showing the EU symbol to the left.

Winter trips demand extra preparation:

- You will need to fit winter tyres for some countries (see ✿ Winter Tyres / ❄ Snow Chains in the checklists in chapters 2-5)
- Your car's battery will be given a real work-out in the cold, so make sure it is in top condition
- Make sure your car's cooling system is filled with the correct strength of antifreeze
- Fill up with winter screenwash, and consider fitting winter wiper blades
- For diesel-engined vehicles, use winter diesel, which is designed for temperatures below freezing
- Apply lubricant to the door seals to prevent them freezing shut

Check the engine thoroughly before your trip.

Topping-up with winter screenwash. (Courtesy ADAC)

What to take:
documents and equipment

Here you'll find plenty of general guidance to help you … you'll find even greater detail in the checklist for each country.

Driving licence

In most European countries, you must have your licence with you at all times. It must be a full, current licence. It's a good idea for one of your passengers to take their licence too, in case of emergencies. If you're hiring a car, check the minimum age requirement, and what proof of your driving record the rental company requires.

International Driving Permit (IDP)

If you hold a non-EU licence, or plan on travelling outside the European Union, an IDP is generally helpful, and often a legal requirement. It can be obtained from national motoring organisations. You must be at least 18 and hold a full national licence. In some countries, you can only use an IDP for stays of 90 days or less.

Be ready to have your licence checked. (Courtesy iStock.com/ Todor Tsvetkov)

Vehicle registration certificate

Take the original registration certificate (in the UK, the V5C). If you're driving someone else's car, get a letter of authorisation from the owner; for hired vehicles, ask the hire company to provide a Vehicle on Hire certificate (in the UK, a VE103 form).

Vehicle insurance

A 'Green Card' is widely recognised as proof that your car meets the minimum requirements for third-party insurance, and is a legal requirement in some countries, particularly in Central & Eastern Europe. If you have comprehensive insurance at home, you'll probably need to pay an extra premium to extend this cover to additional countries. Ask your insurer for this, and a standard 'European Accident Statement' form.

Vehicle breakdown cover

Even if your car is under warranty, check the cover abroad carefully. All the major motoring organisations, and many insurers, can provide comprehensive breakdown assistance, including recovery back to your home.

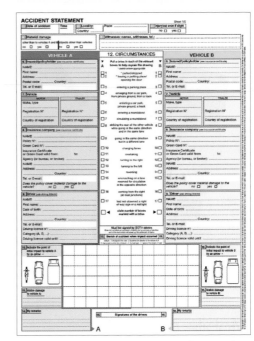

European Accident Statement form.

Don't forget to take a list of service agents for your destination: the manufacturer's website or your local dealer should be able to supply this. Don't rely on the information from a built-in satnav: if your car won't start, you may not be able to access it!

Passports and visas

Make sure that your passport is valid, preferably for six months after your departure date. For destinations outside the EU, check with the embassy or – for UK citizens – the Foreign & Commonwealth website (www.gov. uk/foreign-travel-advice) to see if you need a visa.

Medical cover

For travel within the EU, the EHIC (European Health Insurance Card) will ensure all EU citizens receive treatment, and are reimbursed for many charges. You can usually obtain this online.

Work safely beside your car with a reflective jacket. (Courtesy TCS)

European Touring Kit: all you need for your trip. (Courtesy Ring Automotive Ltd)

Make sure other road users see your car. (Courtesy ÖAMTC)

The EHIC won't cover everything, though, especially if you need treatment in a private clinic. Travel insurance will give you extra peace of mind, and should be considered essential for non-EU citizens and for all travellers outside the EU. Take a copy of any current prescriptions, too.

Mobile phone

Even if you don't normally use one, or are concerned about call charges away from home, a mobile phone can be a godsend if you break down, or to photograph an accident. Consider buying a pay-as-you-go SIM card locally to keep down costs.

☑ Checklist: In the car

Full details of the **legal requirements can be found in the country checklists**, but wherever you go, **it makes sense to take all these items**:

- ☐ **Reflective jacket** for driver and all passengers (**inside the car**)
- ☐ **Emergency warning triangle** (two are often needed when towing)
- ☐ **Fire extinguisher**
- ☐ **First-aid kit**
- ☐ Set of **spare bulbs** (except for xenon or LED lights)
- ☐ **Second** set of **car keys**
- ☐ **Basic tool kit** or **multi-tool**
- ☐ **Blanket** and **torch**
- ☐ **Parking disc**

You can buy convenient kits with the equipment you need from the main motoring organisations, accessory shops or at many ports.

Insurance and breakdown cover

Nobody wants to have an accident or breakdown, and it's easy to begrudge the extra cost of insurance cover, but skimping on this can be a false economy.

A comprehensive travel insurance policy will give you the reassurance that most or all of your costs will be covered, and it can be less stressful dealing with helpline staff who speak your language.

Let's hope it never comes to this! (Courtesy ADAC)

The major motoring organisations at home, and some insurers, offer packages which combine breakdown and accident insurance, covering you and your car throughout Europe. Depending on your needs, you can opt for single-trip or year-round policies; the latter are often better value if you travel regularly to other countries. Most policies include repatriation of your family or friends, if that is needed.

Knowing that your car will be transported home if it can't be repaired locally is also reassuring, especially if you have an older car: in 2013, 70% of the cars repatriated by one major motoring organisation were over five years old. The same applies to less common makes (eg, Lotus or TVR), for which there are fewer service agents abroad. In some countries, including France, you have to pay an officially designated recovery company to tow your car off the motorway, and some insurance companies will let you recoup that cost.

Recovering your car from floodwater can be a stressful experience. (Courtesy ADAC)

Further information

Available from your national motoring organisations. For example –

AA	www.theaa.com/european-breakdown-cover
AAA	www.aaa.com/PPInternational/Benefits_AAA_to_Intl.html
Green Flag	www.greenflag.com/breakdown-cover/european
RAC	www.rac.co.uk/breakdown-cover

Insurance and breakdown cover

Crossing the Channel

Each year more than four million motorists cross the English Channel: travelling with your own car has many advantages.

Taking your own car means that you get the chance to choose your route and take more luggage, and, despite some recent consolidation of the services offered, travellers to and from the UK still have a great choice of crossings.

From Scotland or northern England, the routes from Newcastle and Hull save time on the road, whilst the longer crossings in the western Channel provide a gateway to western France and northern Spain.

The longer crossings are much more expensive, but the latest ships are comfortable and well-equipped. If you are worried about becoming seasick, consider taking an overnight crossing and getting to sleep before the ship even leaves the coast!

For the short crossings in the eastern Channel, Le Shuttle and the traditional ferries each have their fans. The Eurotunnel trains are impervious to choppy seas and the journey time is much shorter. The ferries, on the other hand, give you the chance to relax or shop. On the train, take care not to scuff your wheels if you have a particularly wide car. On the ferry, watch out when boarding if you have a low-slung sports car: drive on at an angle if necessary.

If you have an especially valuable car, try to avoid the open deck spaces, where your car may be lashed by saltwater spray.

You'll find more details in the Port information sections for each relevant country, later in the guide.

Easy self-service check-in for Le Shuttle. (Courtesy Eurotunnel)

Participants in a charity fundraising run drive on board at Dover. (Courtesy Port of Dover)

One of DFDS Seaways' ships in port at Dover. (Courtesy DFDS Seaways)

Filling up

If you're travelling in Western Europe in a recent petrol or diesel car, you should have few worries.

Whatever your fuel, taking some spare cash is a good precaution, as some garages and self-service pumps won't accept credit cards issued in all countries.

For petrol (gasoline) engines, E10 fuel – with 10% ethanol – is increasingly common, but this can be used in most cars built after 2000. In the Netherlands, E15 petrol – with 15% ethanol – is being introduced, so check if it's suitable for your car. In Eastern Europe, and in some areas elsewhere, 98 octane petrol is hard to find. If you have a classic car which requires leaded fuel, take a good supply of additive.

Emptying the tank after filling up with the wrong fuel: a costly mistake you need to address at once. (Courtesy TCS)

For diesel engines, some countries (including France and Germany) are bringing in B7 and B8 biodiesel: check to see if your car can run on these. Winter diesel will keep your engine running down to -20°C (-4°F) or lower.

For a long trip, the lower price of LPG is very attractive. But don't be caught without the right type of filling adapter, as there are several different fitments in use, including

Electric cars like this Fisker Karma are still a rare sight.

'ACME,' bayonet, and 'Euronozzle' models. The website at www.mylpg.eu has full details on which adapter you'll need, and a map of LPG filling stations.

Bioethanol (E85) is also relatively cheap, but in many countries there are few filling stations. Check online at www.fuelcat.de/petrol-stationsin-europe.html for coverage along your route.

Finally, if you have an electric car, think hard before making a long trip, and check the map of charger locations at http://chargemap.com.

Scan the QR codes for further information for your fuel type ...

 LPG

 Bioethanol (E85)

 Electric

Planning your route

Planning your route in advance will reduce the stress of driving on unfamiliar roads, and help you enjoy the journey.

For many travellers, there's little to beat looking at a printed map. Often the best maps are produced locally: by the IGN in France, Touring Club Italiano in Italy, or Kümmerly & Frey in Switzerland, for example. Or you may prefer the consistent style of maps from a single cartographer, such as Michelin.

You don't have to rely on paper when preparing your trip. There are many excellent online services available free of charge: these include Google Maps, Bing Maps, TomTom and Here.com. The last two even let you send your route direct to your satnav. If you're driving through France, ViaMichelin (www.viamichelin.co.uk) provides great coverage, with options to include motorways or take a scenic route. You'll also find many suggestions

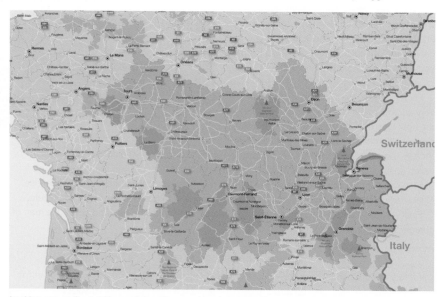

Looking across Central France & the Alps: great touring country!

Clear signposting on the French autoroute, heading down from Calais. (Courtesy Groupe SANEF – Alain Hatat)

Obligatory vignette (toll charge) on this Austrian motorway. (Courtesy ÖAMTC)

for touring itineraries online, notably on motorcycle enthusiast sites, ready to download to popular satnav devices.

The majority of motorists nowadays use some form of satnav, which will be especially useful in an unfamiliar region. Before you leave, make sure you have the latest maps for the countries you'll be visiting. Familiarise yourself in advance with the names of places which change from one language to another – Lille/Rijsel, Genf/Genève and Donostia/San Sebastián, for example – or which will appear in non-Latin script (eg Αθήνα for Athens). If you use a satnav app on your smartphone, download the maps you'll need in advance to avoid costly connection charges. You can also adjust the average speed to suit higher motorway speeds (as in Germany) or slower mountain roads.

Once on the road, let your satnav help you: zoom-in close to be warned of upcoming hairpin bends in the mountains, or zoom out so you can slow down before an unlit village at night. Traffic information programmes on the radio (such as 107.7 FM on French autoroutes) or community traffic services like Waze will also help manage your journey. You'll find more details of these services – and of local tolls – in the country sections later in the guide.

Choosing route options on a Volvo Sensus satnav.

TomTom satnav integrated into Renault's in-car system. (Courtesy TomTom)

Planning your route

Driving safety and hazards

Inevitably when driving in another country, you will find yourself in unfamiliar situations. Many countries – including Sweden, the UK and the Netherlands – enjoy low accident rates, and drivers there are generally disciplined and courteous.

In other countries, drivers take a more relaxed attitude to rules and regulations, which can be unnerving for the visitor. Wherever you drive, however, the basic precepts of safe driving will serve you well: be alert to other road users and anticipate what they may do; slow down and keep your distance, even when the locals conspicuously fail to do so!

Many rules should be followed everywhere:

A humorous approach to a serious topic: a campaign to encourage young road users to belt up. (Courtesy YOURS)

- **Seat belts** should **always be used** when fitted, by both front and rear seat passengers
- **Crash helmets** should **always be worn** by motorcyclists
- **Drink-driving limits** vary by country and may be lower than at home, but the **only safe rule is never to mix the two**
- **Drugs and medicines** should also be **avoided**, many of which can have **side-effects** such as causing drowsiness

The STOP sign, seen here in Austria, is universal. (Courtesy ÖAMTC) / Headlights illuminate an animal at the side of the road. (Courtesy ADAC)

Many of the country sections which follow feature illustrations of unusual road signs, but most signs follow international conventions. The shape of both the 'Stop' sign (an octagon) and the 'Give Way' sign (an inverted triangle) are the same everywhere, so that they can be recognised even when covered in snow.

Weather and the seasons

There is more information about driving in winter on pages 38-41, but each season brings its own challenges. One recent study found that October was the most dangerous month on the roads, with fog and slippery autumn leaves to contend with. Wild animals often come out then,

Beware of autumn leaves, especially if on a motorcycle! (Courtesy ADAC)

Driving safety and hazards

23

too, particularly at dusk, so be ready to slow for them on country roads. Using main beam headlights may cause them to freeze in their tracks.

In regions such as northern Italy, fog is certainly one of the greatest dangers: leave plenty of space ahead of you and keep your speed right down. In France, there is an overall 50km/h speed limit in fog, on all types of road. Use your dipped headlights and rear fog lamps to make your vehicle more easily seen; at blind junctions, flash your lights and sound your horn to signal your presence. Using your wipers will help keep your screen clear.

Fog is one of the worst conditions to drive in. (Courtesy ADAC)

Low sunlight can also impair visibility: be sure to keep your windows clean and free from smears.

In the spring, the roads can be flooded after winter snows melt: don't drive on if you can't see how deep the water is. If you can, drive through at a steady speed, keeping to the middle of the road if possible, as this is often highest, and be sure to check your brakes afterwards. On major

When the sun is low, use the sun visors and ensure the windscreen is clean. (Courtesy ADAC)

Aquaplaning is a major risk on surfaces this wet. (Courtesy TCS)

roads, surface water can cause aquaplaning, whilst wet weather often leads to poor visibility.

High winds can occur at any time of year: take special care when overtaking high-sided vehicles, or if you have a roof load or trailer yourself, and keep your speed down on exposed bridges.

Wet weather makes for reduced visibility, with lots of spray on this French motorway.

Driving safety and hazards

The other side of the road

For British and Irish motorists visiting Continental Europe, driving on the opposite side of the road is by far the biggest cause of concern. First-time visitors to the UK or Ireland from North America, France or Germany will be just as disconcerted.

The good news is that after a short period of adjustment, most drivers find it much less difficult than they feared. And if you plan on renting a car in Europe, the control layout is the same for left and right-hand drive cars.

90% of the world's traffic is in countries which drive on the right, and in Europe, only the UK, Ireland, Malta and Cyprus drive on the left – all of them islands. Since Sweden changed over in 1967, there are now no places in Europe where drivers have to change sides at a border crossing.

Keeping to the correct side of the road soon becomes second nature.
(Courtesy ASFINAG/Wolfgang Simlinger)

A French-registered MG on a deserted road in Scotland. / Watch out when leaving a single-lane track to rejoin a main road. (Courtesy Tourism Ireland)

On the other side of the road: what to look out for

Once you're in the flow of traffic, it soon becomes natural to keep to the correct side of the road. The greatest risks are when re-joining an empty road, after a stop at a filling station or car park, or when starting out for the first time each day. Roundabouts can be especially disorienting: increasingly – and unless otherwise signposted – the rule is to give way to traffic already on the roundabout. In many Continental countries, and not just France, traffic from the right has priority: take special care in towns.

If you are driving a right-hand drive car on the Continent, or a left-hand drive car in the UK or Ireland, for example, take special care when changing lanes on a motorway, and make good use of both exterior mirrors. If your car is equipped with a blind spot detection system, this can be a boon. Don't hog the centre or overtaking lanes if you're not actually overtaking, and pull back in after completing the manoeuvre. In many countries, including France, it is compulsory to indicate when pulling in as well as out.

For North American visitors to Europe

'Undertaking' (ie, passing on the right in Continental Europe, or the left in the UK and Ireland) is generally prohibited.

At junctions with traffic lights, turning right on red is also forbidden, unless there is a separate filter arrow allowing you to do so.

Left- or right-hand drive: the controls are the same, as shown in this Honda Accord.

Traffic offences in Europe

With so many driving laws being the same across the European Union, it's surprising how many differences still exist in speed limits and other traffic legislation.

In the past few years, however, the EU has taken major steps to coordinate its procedures for pursuing traffic offenders across Europe, with the UK and Ireland falling in line by 2017.

Mobile speed check in Austria. (Courtesy ÖAMTC)

In many countries, the police can issue on-the-spot fines, which must often be paid immediately. Where that's not possible (for example, for speeding caught on camera), the police can now take action against offenders in their home country, and you will receive the ticket in the mail! Users of hire cars will no longer escape, either, as the rental companies now have a legal obligation to supply the hirer's details to the police. At present, points will not be deducted from foreign driving licences, but, for particularly serious offences, the police can suspend your licence in the country you are visiting. Fines abroad can be much higher, especially in countries like Finland, which base the amount on the offender's personal income.

At the same time, legislation covering the use of radar detectors has been introduced, with many countries outlawing their use, as well as POI-based alerts on satnav devices (see chapters 2-5).

For parking offences, many countries are tightening up their procedures. More than 400 cities now routinely use international debt collection agencies to pursue unpaid parking tickets, with the fine increased if it's not paid promptly. You have been warned!

A forgotten parking ticket can follow you home. (Courtesy ÖAMTC)

Disabled travellers

Crossing the Channel

Being disabled needn't prevent you enjoying a trip by car to another country. All the ferry operators will be happy to help disabled passengers, but book well in advance and arrive early at the port, so that you can be sure to get a parking space or cabin near the lifts. Nearly all their ships have been adapted for wheelchair access, with passenger lifts, disabled toilets, and specially adapted cabins on overnight sailings. If you prefer to take Le Shuttle, you can remain in your own car during the journey, although there are no disabled toilets on the trains.

Assistance dogs for blind passengers are also welcome on board, and usually travel free, but, like all pets, they must be registered (see page 31). If you have a hearing impairment, let the ship's staff know, so that they can ensure you receive all the information from onboard announcements.

The wheelchair symbol is universally recognised.

While you are abroad

The 'Blue Badge' sign for disabled drivers is widely recognised across Europe, and visitors should enjoy the same rights as local residents. In some cities (eg, Paris) parking will be free, in other places you'll need to pay, so check the local signs. Check, too, whether you need to display a parking disc showing your arrival time,, and whether access restrictions (such as the 'ZTL' in Italy, see page 92) also apply to disabled drivers. You will find lots more information for each country at www.disabledmotorists.eu, including guidance for visitors from outside the EU.

You may still need to use a parking disc.

Scan the QR code for further info ...

Most port terminals have excellent facilities for the disabled, as here at Portsmouth. (Courtesy Portsmouth Port)

Disabled travellers

Travelling with children

A trip across Europe can be a great experience for all the family, and a real adventure for your children.

You may be travelling longer distances than they are used to, so be sure to have plenty to keep them occupied. Side window blinds will help them stay comfortable in the summer sun. Several EU countries are introducing legislation forbidding smoking in cars in which children are carried.

These children have well-fitting seats and plenty of toys to keep them safe and happy. (Courtesy ADAC)

But your children's safety is sure to be your main concern. Take just as much care as you would back home, even if the locals don't always seem to bother with child seats or other restraints. The exact rules vary by country (see the checklists in chapters 2-5), but nearly all countries require children to be securely held in place with child seats or other restraints appropriate to their age, height or weight. In general, children under three should travel in the rear seats. If you are using a rearward-facing carrier in the front, remember to disable the passenger airbag. Otherwise, children may only use the front passenger seat once they reach a specified minimum age, height or weight. As well as securing your children safely, make sure that holiday luggage can't be thrown towards them if you have to brake suddenly.

If you are hiring a car, the same rules apply, so check in advance what safety equipment, such as an approved child seat or restraint, will be provided. You may feel more comfortable bringing your child's usual seat from home.

Take care when fitting a child seat in an unfamiliar car. (Courtesy TCS)

Travelling with pets

Taking your pet abroad

Gone are the days when taking a foreign holiday meant leaving behind your pet. The Pet Travel Scheme (PETS) lets your dog, cat, or ferret travel with you in the European Union without spending time in quarantine. You will need to obtain a pet passport, and have your pet microchipped and vaccinated against rabies. For UK travellers, for example, the UK Government website, at www.gov.uk/take-pet-abroad, explains what you need to do, and provides information on the rules for other animals, and for travel to non-EU countries. Your vet will tell you how to protect your pet from diseases such as leishmaniasis in other parts of Europe.

In the car

Keeping your pet safe and comfortable will be your main concern on the road. You may be carrying a lot more luggage than usual, so consider using a divider in the luggage compartment, or adding a roof box for luggage, to give your dog a decent amount of space. A few manufacturers sell special dog harnesses to use in conjunction with the car's seat belts. Alternatively, you may want to invest in a cage to use in the luggage compartment, or – for cats and smaller dogs – on the rear seat. Some countries, such as Italy, have specific legislation to ensure that animals are carried securely.

Temperatures in southern Europe can be very high, so remember to stop often and give your pet plenty of water and time to run around. Carrying a pet first-aid kit will help you deal with minor emergencies.

More than a million dogs, cats and ferrets have taken Le Shuttle. (Courtesy Eurotunnel)

This 'Dog Bag' is ideal for carrying this dog in his Mercedes. (Courtesy www.roofbox.co.uk)

Travelling with pets

Towing abroad and holiday loads

Loading up

One of the great advantages of travelling by car is that you can take far more luggage with you than you would if flying. But that holiday load can put an extra strain on your car, increasing stopping distances and affecting handling. When packing for your trip, try and keep heavy loads low down, and remember the extra weight of that wine and beer! Keep loose objects secure with luggage nets and don't pile up the rear parcel shelf: objects

Heavy luggage on the roof raises the car's centre of gravity and affects handling. (Courtesy TCS)

placed there will block your view and can be thrown forward if you have to brake hard.

A roof box is a good way of adding luggage space, but try and place lighter soft bags in it, and don't forget the extra height in car parks and tunnels, and when booking space on the ferry. If you have a cycle carrier or other overhanging load at the rear of the vehicle, make sure that your lights and number plate remain clearly visible: you may need to add a repeater panel. In some countries, including Italy and Spain, it's a legal requirement to use a red and white striped panel (50cm by 50cm in size) when carrying overhanging loads.

Keep luggage secure inside the car. (Courtesy ADAC)

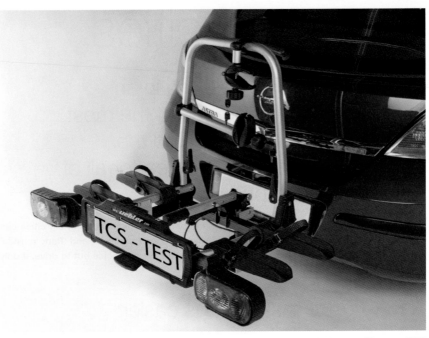

This cycle carrier fits securely and ensures the car's lights can still be seen. (Courtesy TCS)

Towing

If you have never towed on the other side of the road, it can take time to adjust to the different angles when turning, and especially when reversing. Local clubs – such as the Caravan Club in the UK (www.caravanclub.co.uk) – sometimes run courses which you can take before you go. Clubs like these also provide lots of good information on speed limits and other restrictions when towing, taking account of the weight of the towing vehicle and its maximum towing limit. These rules are complex, especially in France, so take the time to check for your particular outfit. Lower speed limits will often be signposted for hills and roads which are exposed to crosswinds. In Germany, you may tow at a higher speed (100km/h) if your outfit passes a TÜV stability test.

Towing abroad: extension mirrors are essential. (Courtesy The Caravan Club)

A Camping Card International (CCI) is a convenient ID to use at campsites across Europe, and is a legal requirement in Denmark.

Driving in cities

For many motorists, driving in an unfamiliar city can be one of the most stressful experiences behind the wheel, epitomised by the free-for-all of the Arc de Triomphe in Paris!

With heavy traffic, unfamiliar street signs, and impatient locals all around, big cities can be exhausting to drive in. Public transport – which is often excellent – and 'Park 'n' Ride' schemes are a great alternative, but sometimes you'll have no choice but to drive, if only to reach your hotel.

A few tips to make things easier:

- **Stay calm** and don't be flustered by impatient local drivers
- Turn off your radio, so you can **concentrate** fully on your driving
- If you have one, **program your satnav in advance** and use POI features to find car parks and other key locations
- Even if you have a satnav, however, make sure to **look at your route in advance**: **familiarise yourself** with key intersections or districts which you will pass through. In countries such as the Netherlands, these districts may be numbered

Foreign street signs can seem bewildering. / Look out for pedestrians and children, especially near stationary buses and coaches. (Both courtesy ÖAMTC)

Narrow streets, parked cars, and cyclists: plenty to watch out for! (Courtesy ÖAMTC)

Paying the Congestion Charge in central London. (Courtesy ÖAMTC)

● In France, look for the *'Toutes Directions'* signs to find your way out of the city, and then pick up the signs to your destination

● **Take special care at junctions and roundabouts**, where local rules – or simply accepted practices – often apply. Some of these – such as giving way to traffic already on a roundabout, or turning in front of cars turning left from the other lane – are covered in the country sections which follow

● **Make full use of your indicators** when changing lanes or direction, even if the drivers around you seem not to bother

● Watch out for bus lanes, which sometimes operate only during peak hours

● More and more European cities are introducing **restrictions** or **charges** to enter central areas, to reduce the amount of traffic and lower emissions. Italy has restricted access zones ('ZTL') in many historic sites, whilst in Germany, 50 towns have environmental zones that require a windscreen sticker to enter. In the UK, central London has a Congestion Charge; Paris is progressively extending limitations on older vehicles which pollute more.

Driving in a foreign country

Driving in the mountains

For the motoring enthusiast, there is little to beat the exhilaration of driving over some of Europe's most beautiful mountain roads.

Often superbly engineered, these Alpine passes reach as high as 2800m (9200ft). Once the stage for sporting events like the Coupe des Alpes, they now attract drivers from across Europe.

For once, drivers of right-hand drive cars need not be at a disadvantage, with the closest possible view of the road edge. Indeed, many prewar French and Italian touring cars were right-hand drive for just this reason. Even so, mountain roads, with their multiple hairpin bends, demand extra care, especially at night. Vehicles coming uphill usually have priority, and there are special rules in countries such as Austria and Switzerland which favour postal buses. Be sure to select your gears appropriately, using lower gears not just when climbing, but to provide additional engine braking when coming down. In cars with automatic transmission, use

The beautiful Gorge de la Truyère in France.

Driving in the mountains

Snow posts mark the edge of the road up to Mont Ventoux in winter.

the sport or manual modes for extra control. Watch, too, for brake fade and possible overheating, especially if your car is fully loaded or towing.

Many mountain passes are open for only limited periods each year: see the 'Mountains' sections in the country pages for Austria, France, Italy and Switzerland which follow, for full details of opening periods, gradients and tolls, and whether they may be used by caravans.

Tunnels

At other times of year – or if you are in a hurry to reach your final destination – road and Motorail tunnels provide a fast and safe alternative to many of the major passes. Road tunnels are often much longer than you may be used to, and you may find it tiring, as your eyes adjust to changes in the light. Be sure to switch on your headlights and keep a safe distance from the vehicle in front of you. Keep an eye on your speed too, as some tunnels – like those between Genoa and Nice – can be surprisingly twisty. Stop only in an emergency, and, if you have to, switch off your engine and follow the signs to the nearest emergency exit.

Loose rocks can be a danger on mountain roads, like this one in Spain. (Courtesy Daniel Ernst/ Thinkstock)

Sophisticated control room for the Plabutschtunnel on the A9 autobahn, Austria. (Courtesy ASFINAG/ Wolfgang Simlinger)

Winter driving: equipment

If there's just one thing you should do to keep going in winter conditions, it's fit winter tyres to your car.

Specially designed to work not just on snow and ice, but in all conditions under 7°C (45°F), winter tyres provide much better grip, improving traction and greatly reducing stopping distances. They're compulsory in many European countries (see the checklists in chapters 2-5), and you may be fined if your car isn't correctly equipped.

All new cars registered in the EU and Switzerland since November 2014 must be fitted with a tyre pressure monitoring system (TPMS), and that requirement applies to winter tyres as well. If you're hiring a car, make sure it has the correct tyres, too.

When snow or ice covers the road, winter tyres alone may not be enough, in which case you will need to fit studded tyres or snow chains. For occasional use, 'snow socks' are a great alternative to chains, as they are much easier to fit. They are officially accepted as an alternative

Winter tyres have a special compound and tread pattern. (Courtesy ADAC)

You may need snow chains to reach a ski resort. (Courtesy TCS) / 'Snow socks' are easy and quick to fit. (Courtesy www.autosock.co.uk)

on roads where chains are compulsory in France, Germany and the Czech Republic. Whichever you use, stop after a few miles and make sure they are still secure. Watch for local speed limit signs: in many countries, cars with snow chains are restricted to 50km/h (31mph). If your car has a traction control system, that should be disabled while you are driving with chains, and they should be removed as soon as you are back on dry tarmac.

This sign indicates that chains must be used on the road ahead.

Winter driving: equipment

☑ Checklist: In the car

Car accessory shops and motoring organisations often sell convenient kits with many of the things you'll need, in case you get stuck, or you can make up your own kit with the following essentials:

- ☐ An **old carpet or mat** to place under the **drive wheels**, to help get started
- ☐ A folding **snow shovel**
- ☐ A **tow rope**
- ☐ **Jump leads**
- ☐ Spare **fuel**
- ☐ An **ice scraper**
- ☐ A **de-icer** spray or WD40®, to open frozen door locks
- ☐ A **torch**, with **spare batteries**
- ☐ A **blanket**
- ☐ Plenty of **warm clothing** and **gloves**
- ☐ A **hot drink** and **energy bars**
- ☐ **Sunglasses**, to reduce the glare from snow

Winter driving: guidance

Driving in some foreign countries in winter – with more severe weather – can be hard on you and your car, with more severe weather than you're used to.

Fortunately, local authorities and drivers are usually much better prepared, and winter conditions cause less disruption. Courses on skid pans, or at ice driving circuits in the French Alps, allow you to practise in safety.

Driving on snow and ice can be disconcerting at first. Listen to local travel information, and plan your route to keep to main roads, if you can. When you start off each day, allow plenty of time to clear snow off the car: snow on the roof may fall into your path, or that of other vehicles.

The secret to making safe progress is to drive smoothly: avoid sudden braking, changes of direction and acceleration. When starting off, using second gear will help you gain traction; in cars with automatic transmissions, use the winter mode, if fitted, or select the highest gear

Snow on each side of the Pas de la Casa, Andorra. (Courtesy Andorra Turisme)

Clearing heavy snow on an Austrian motorway. (Courtesy ASFINAG/Wolfgang Simlinger) / 'Glatteis': German for dangerous black ice. (Courtesy ÖAMTC)

possible in manual mode. Keep your headlights on, and be sure to keep your windows clear of ice, using the air-conditioning to reduce the build-up of humidity. If your car's suspension lets you change the ride height, choose the highest position to prevent your car sliding toboggan-like over the snow.

Allow plenty of space around you, and moderate your speed, as it will take much longer to stop than on dry roads; use engine braking to help slow down. If your car does not have ABS brakes, cadence braking – rhythmically pumping your foot up and down on the brake pedal – will prevent the wheels locking up. If you do get into a skid, avoid hard braking and steer gently in the direction you want to go. In a rear-wheel drive car, ease off the throttle. If you start to slide down a hill, turn the steering full on and apply the handbrake. The rear wheels will lock and a block of snow will form ahead of your front wheels, so slowing you down.

Finally, when you get home, wash the underbody of your car to remove the build-up of corrosive salt.

Salt helps keep the roads clear of ice, but can damage your car. (Courtesy ASFINAG/Wolfgang Simlinger)

Winter driving: guidance

Heading further afield

The spectacular Transfăgărăşan Highway in Romania. (Courtesy Romania Tourism)

If you're planning to drive to one of the Eastern European countries, it probably won't be your first long road trip. But you may be flying there for work, or on holiday, and need to get around in a hire car.

Most national governments offer advice to their citizens travelling abroad, highlighting any health or security concerns. UK citizens, for instance, can check www.gov.uk/foreign-travel-advice. In several of these countries, the languages spoken use Cyrillic or other non-Latin alphabets, so a phrasebook (or smartphone app) will come in handy.

For motorists, road conditions remain variable, but are steadily improving, with European-funded road-building programmes in the Baltic States, Albania and Romania, for example. In places such as Slovenia, the roads are just as good as in many Western European countries. Accident rates remain high in countries like Poland or Russia, but the authorities are making a lot of progress to bring them down.

The checklists in chapter 5 provide more details of the exact requirements in each country, but comprehensive accident and breakdown insurance should be considered a must, as should an insurance Green Card. An International Driving Permit (IDP) will be needed more often, and you may require a 'Carnet de Passage en Douane' (see pages 44-45) and International Certificate for Motor Vehicles (ICMV) – a translation of your vehicle registration document, available from the AA in the UK – to facilitate border crossings in some places. A set of basic spares is well worth packing too.

A flooded road in Estonia. (Courtesy Welcome to Estonia/ Jarek JYepera)

Scan the QR codes for further travel advice

UK Gov

AA (ICMV)

Taking an historic vehicle abroad

For many classic car enthusiasts, taking their car to another country is a highlight of the year, whether to tour unspoilt countryside or join in a local event.

You can find out more about events in France in the author's book, *France: The Essential Guide for Car Enthusiasts*. Magazines such as *MotorKlassik* in Germany and *RuoteClassiche* in Italy are also great sources of inspiration.

For a first journey abroad, a trip organised by a specialist tour operator can provide extra peace of mind, but you may prefer the flexibility of setting your own route. Whichever you choose, it's important to give your car a thorough check over before you leave, and to have insurance including recovery of your car back home.

Many classic car owners will always carry a basic set of tools and spares, and that is definitely recommended on longer trips abroad. If you belong to a club for your marque of car, check in advance to see if there is a similar club in the country you are visiting. They will often be able to assist you in finding a garage specialising in your model of car, to provide parts or help in an emergency.

Happily, historic vehicles are involved in relatively few accidents, but check to see if any special regulations apply. In France, for example, front seat belts must be fitted and used in cars built after July 1973, whilst children under three may only be carried if an appropriate restraint is fitted.

An English MGA roadster in a village near Angoulême.

British participants prepare to take the honours in a concours d'élégance at Deauville.

Taking an historic vehicle abroad

Longer stays abroad vertical sidebar text on left margin.

Longer stays abroad

For most holiday and business trips, you can use your own car throughout Europe with few formalities.

In Russia and some countries beyond the European Union, however, it makes sense to check with the embassy for longer stays, or if you're bringing in a high-value car. Although not mandatory, a 'Carnet de Passage en Douane' – available from the RAC in the UK – may be helpful: this is an internationally recognised Customs document which lets you import a vehicle temporarily. Different versions allow five, ten or 25 border crossings. You will need to pay an administrative fee and a (returnable) security deposit.

For tourists from outside the EU, three special schemes, Citroën Europass, Peugeot Open Europe and Renault Eurodrive, enable you to lease a brand-new car for a period of three weeks to six months; at the end, you can buy the car or simply return it. You can use the car throughout Europe, and it offers better value than conventional car hire.

A Peugeot 5008: a spacious and comfortable car in which to tour Europe. (Courtesy Peugeot)

The Carnet de Passages en Douane. (Courtesy FIA/AIT)

Within the EU, you may use your own car abroad for up to six months, or – for registered students in all EU member states except Denmark – for as long as you are studying there. EU citizens can use their national driving licence indefinitely in another EU country, but visitors from outside the EU must apply for a new licence locally after 12 months, and you may be required to take a driving test. Check too with your insurer about extending your cover.

If you're planning to make an extended stay or move abroad permanently, you'll need to re-register your car in your new country. This can be a complex process, and it may make more sense to buy a new car on arrival. Right-hand drive (RHD) cars will be less convenient to drive, especially when overtaking or at parking barriers. In Croatia, Lithuania, Poland, Serbia, Slovakia and Ukraine, it's currently forbidden to re-register RHD cars. US cars can also be difficult to register within Europe; as with British cars, specific parts may not be available locally, and they'll be more difficult to sell on.

Not for the faint-hearted! It took the author several months to re-register this American Ford Mustang in France.

Scan the QR code for details of the Carnet de Passage en Douane from the RAC

What to do: accidents and car crime

112: the European-wide emergency service number.

Having an accident whilst on holiday is everyone's worst nightmare, but if the worst does happen, your first priority is the safety of your passengers.

If you need medical help, call the emergency services at once: the 112 number is used throughout the European Union, and in most countries beyond it. Medical services are excellent in most European countries and doctors usually speak some English.

If you can, move your car and passengers to a place of safety off the road, to avoid further accidents. Don't forget to put on your reflective jacket and place a warning triangle at least 50m behind your vehicle.

Recovering a car after an accident. (Courtesy ÖAMTC/Petra Spiola)

You should always call the police in the following circumstances:

- If any **people** or **animals** are **injured**
- If any **vehicles** are **blocking the road**
- If any **vehicles** are **seriously damaged**, as they may not be safe to drive
- If you suspect any of the **drivers** of being **under the influence of drink or drugs**
- If the **drivers** involved **disagree** about what happened

In most countries, both drivers normally complete a European Accident Statement Form – which your insurer should provide – as a record of what happened. Electronic forms are being introduced in France, but are not yet accepted by foreign insurers, so stick to paper for now. Be sure to report the accident to your insurer (and rental company for hire cars) as soon as possible.

A fire crew uses sophisticated cutting equipment on a BMW i3 electric car. (Courtesy ADAC)

Taking a photo with your smartphone or camera can be helpful, but the use of dashcams is not recommended in Belgium, Germany, Luxembourg, Portugal, Sweden or Switzerland on data privacy grounds; in Austria you must have a special permit. Drivers in southern Europe, especially, often seem impatient and reckless: stay calm and don't give in to road rage. If you are the victim of road rage yourself, avoid eye contact and, above all, don't attempt to retaliate.

Car crime

Always keep your car locked and your valuables out of sight, not just when parked, but at filling stations and in slow-moving traffic, too. Beware of scams, with people running into you at junctions or flagging you down for help with supposed breakdowns.

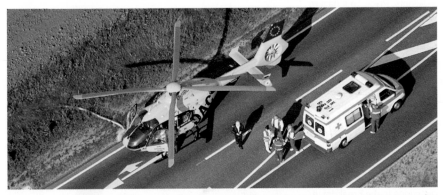

The German ADAC organisation can call on a fleet of air ambulances for critical emergencies. (Courtesy ADAC)

What to do: accidents and car crime

What to do: breakdowns

Breaking down whilst abroad is a major worry for many motorists.

Ensuring your car is well prepared (see page 12) will help reduce the chances of breaking down – but punctures and unexpected mechanical failures can still happen.

Being clearly seen is even more important at night. (Courtesy ÖAMTC)

Move your car to a layby or the side of the road if you can, and get your passengers to a place of safety. Put on your reflective jacket as soon as you leave the car, and switch on your hazard warning lights and/or sidelights. Place your hazard warning triangle at least 50m behind your vehicle.

Keeping a fully charged mobile phone with you will make it easier to call for help from your insurance provider or car manufacturer (for new cars under warranty). Many satnav systems let you check the exact GPS coordinates of your location, making it easier for you to give exact directions to the breakdown service.

Breakdowns are worse still in winter. (Courtesy ÖAMTC)

Get to a service station for help, if you can. (Courtesy robwilson39/Thinkstock)

On the motorway

All too many deaths on motorways involve a stationary vehicle, so try first of all to get off the motorway if you can. If you sense something is wrong with your vehicle, try and reach the next exit or rest area, but don't take any unnecessary risks if you're worried about the brakes or steering. If you do have to stop on the hard shoulder, stop as far from the passing traffic as you can, with your front wheels pointing ahead or away from the flow of traffic. Leave the car on the right-hand side on the Continent, or the left-hand side in countries which drive on the left. Get all your passengers behind the crash barrier or onto the embankment. Use the nearest emergency phone to call for help, rather than your mobile phone. In several countries, including France, you will have to use the designated breakdown service to recover your vehicle off the motorway, before you can use your manufacturer or insurer's policy. Don't try to repair any problems yourself: it's much too dangerous with cars rushing close by at 80mph (130km/h) or more.

Modern engines are very complex: don't attempt to repair them on the motorway yourself.

I spy ...
international registration codes

Since the expansion of the European Union in 2004, it has become much more common to see cars, lorries and coaches from across Europe on the road.

This list shows you where they come from, which countries are members of the European Union (EU), and which countries use the Euro, or their own, national currency.

Code	Country	Currency
AL	Albania	Lek (ALL)
AND	Andorra	Euro (EUR)
AM	Armenia	Dram (AMD)
A	Austria	Euro (EUR)
AZ	Azerbaijan	New Manat (AZN)
BY	Belarus	Ruble (BYR)
B	Belgium	Euro (EUR)
BIH	Bosnia-Herzegovina	Marka (BAM)
BG	Bulgaria	Lev (BGN)
HR	Croatia	Kuna (HRK)
CY	Cyprus	Euro (EUR)
CZ	Czech Republic	Koruna (CZK)
DK	Denmark	Krone (DKK)
EST	Estonia	Euro (EUR)
FIN	Finland	Euro (EUR)
F	France	Euro (EUR)
GE	Georgia	Lari (GEL)
DE	Germany	Euro (EUR)
GBZ	Gibraltar	Gibraltar Pound (GIP)
GR	Greece	Euro (EUR)
H	Hungary	Forint (HUF)
IS	Iceland	Krona (ISK)
IRL	Ireland	Euro (EUR)
I	Italy	Euro (EUR)
RKS	Kosovo	Euro (EUR)
LV	Latvia	Euro (EUR)

Code	Country	Currency
FL	Liechtenstein	Swiss Franc (CHF)
LT	Lithuania	Euro (EUR)
L	Luxembourg	Euro (EUR)
MK	Macedonia (FYROM)	Denar (MKD)
M	Malta	Euro (EUR)
MD	Moldova	Leu (MDL)
MC	Monaco	Euro (EUR)
MNE	Montenegro	Euro (EUR)
NL	Netherlands	Euro (EUR)
N	Norway	Krone (NOK)
PL	Poland	Zloty (PLN)
P	Portugal	Euro (EUR)
RO	Romania	New Leu (RON)
RUS	Russia	Ruble (RUB)
RSM	San Marino	Euro (EUR)
SRB	Serbia	Dinar (RSD)
SK	Slovakia	Euro (EUR)
SLO	Slovenia	Euro (EUR)
E	Spain	Euro (EUR)
S	Sweden	Krona (SEK)
CH	Switzerland	Swiss Franc (CHF)
TR	Turkey	Lira (TRY)
UA	Ukraine	Hryvnia (UAH)
GB	United Kingdom	British Pound (GBP)
V or SCV	Vatican City	Euro (EUR)

Pale blue rows indicate EU member states

Western Europe

2

Breathtaking mountain scenery: what driving in the Alps is all about.
(Courtesy swiss-images.ch/Markus Buehler)

Austria

Austria is a great destination for the motorist, with stunning mountain roads like the Großglockner. It's also the gateway to other countries in central Europe, including Hungary, the Czech Republic and Slovenia. Roads are generally well maintained and drivers well disciplined, making for a good safety record.

Particularly for visitors less familiar with Alpine roads, driving in the mountains nonetheless requires special care. Buses always have priority, and on single-track roads, the vehicle which can give way more easily should stop.

Austria has an efficient motorway network, and – unlike Germany – there is an overall speed limit, making these roads less intimidating. The 'corridor' toll charge, for drivers travelling straight through Austria, no longer exists, so you will need to buy a 'Vignette,' a windscreen sticker giving you the right to use the motorway network. It's available for periods of ten days or two months, as well as the whole year; provided your car weighs under 3.5 tonnes, it also covers a trailer. On the major routes, traffic news is broadcast every 30 minutes on the Ö3 radio station. If traffic backs up on motorways or other dual carriageways, the queuing cars must create a free lane ('Rettungsgasse') between the lines of vehicles, so that the emergency services can still get through.

In Austria's major cities, traffic restrictions are sometimes imposed when air pollution levels are high. At night, use your sidelights when parking in areas with no street lighting, and check for lampposts with red markings, which indicate that the lights go out at midnight. Vienna has a large central pedestrian area and parking is limited to three hours or less in the short-term parking zones ('Kurzparkzonen'). Salzburg city centre is closed to cars in wet weather during July and August.

The annual 'Vignette' (toll sticker) to use Austria's motorways. (Courtesy ÖAMTC)

The Voralpenkreuz intersection on the A1 autobahn. (Courtesy ASFINAG)

The magnificent Gerlos Alpenstraße. (Courtesy Archiv Großglockner Hochalpenstraßen AG)

No passage for motor vehicles in either direction

No entry for motor vehicles

KURZPARKZONE

Short-term parking zone

auf Pfeifsignal achten

Wait for audible signal before proceeding

ausgenommen Anrainer

Local access only (no through traffic)

Bitte Motor abstellen

Switch off engine

Traffic calming zone: pedestrians may use roadway. 20km/h speed limit

Tram may turn on red or amber signal

SPEED LIMITS

		km/h
Towns/villages	**50** / **30**	in some cities
Main roads	**100**	
Motorways	**130** / **110**	at night in places

GENERAL RULES

Drink-drive limit (g/l blood)	0.5 / 0.1 for novice drivers (first two years)	
Children in front seats	Min 14 yo and 1.5m height, unless suitable restraint used	
Min driving age	18 / 21 to rent car	
Licence or IDP	✓	UK photocard or three-part pink licence recommended
Insurance: Green Card	✓	Recommended
DRL	○	Use in poor visibility
Mobile phones	⊘	Handheld prohibited
	✕	Hands-free tolerated, but not recommended
Radar detectors	⊘	Prohibited
GPS speed camera alerts (POI)	✓	Allowed
Emergency services	Call 112	
Special rules	• Do not overtake stationary school buses • Use of horn prohibited in Vienna and near hospitals • Special permit required to use dashcams	

i www.austria.info/uk/how-to-get-there/austria-by-road-1134817.html

DRIVING EQUIPMENT

Warning triangle	○	Required
High-vis jacket(s)	○	Required
First-aid kit	○	Required
Fire extinguisher	✓	Recommended
Spare bulbs	✓	Recommended
Spare fuel (can)	✓	Permitted (max 10L)
Winter tyres	○	Mandatory 1 Nov–15 Apr Display red sticker if using studded tyres
Snow chains		May be required depending on local conditions

TOLLS

Tolls (Maut) on all motorways and express roads	
How to pay	Vignette (sticker) available for ten days/two months/full year
i	Buy vignette at border, petrol stations, post offices, in advance from motoring organisations, or at www.tolltickets.com

Additional tolls for some mountain roads and tunnels: see *Mountain roads & tunnels* - page 54 Some can be paid in advance with video sticker

Mountain roads and tunnels

Stop ahead to pay the special toll for the Arlberg Schnellstraße. (Courtesy ASFINAG)

KEY 📍→ Location 🏔 Statistics: height m / ft / max gradient 📅 When open 🏷 Toll 🚐 Caravans+trailers *i* Info

 Arlberg Schnellstraße (S16) & Tunnel

📍 St Anton → Langen 🏔 1793 / 5883 / 13% 📅 Some closures Dec to Apr 🏷 Yes (Tunnel) 🚐 Must use Tunnel *i* +43 (0) 5446 226 90

 Brenner Pass (B182) & Autobahn (A13)

📍 Innsbruck → Vipiteno (Italy) 🏔 / 1374 / 4508 / 10% 📅 Normally open all year 🏷 Yes (Autobahn) 🚐 Must use autobahn *i* www.asfinag.at/maut/sonder-und-videomaut

 Felbertauern (B108)

📍 Matrei → Mittersill 🏔 1650 / 5413 / 9% 📅 Normally open all year 🏷 Yes 🚐 May be used *i* www.felbertauernstrasse.at/en

 Flexenstraße (B198/L198)

📍 Stuben → Zürs 🏔 1784 / 5853 / 10% 📅 Some closures Nov to Apr 🏷 No 🚐 Not recommended *i* +43 (0) 5572 232 32 0

 Gerlitzen Panoramastraße

📍 Arriach → Gerlitzen 🏔 1909 / 6263 / 18% 📅 Open May to Oct 🏷 Yes 🚐 Not recommended

 Gerlos Alpenstraße (B165)

📍 Gerlos → Krimml 🏔 1682 / 5518 / 9% 📅 Normally open all year 🏷 Yes 🚐 May be used *i* www.gerlosstrasse.at/en/

 Großglockner Hochalpenstrasse

📍 Bruck → Heiligenblut 🏔 2504 / 8215 / 12% 📅 Open May to Oct; closed at night 🏷 Yes 🚐 Not recommended *i* www.grossglockner.at/en/

 Hochtannberg Pass (L200)

📍 Schröcken → Warth 🏔 1675 / 5495 / 14% 📅 Some closures Jan to Mar 🏷 No 🚐 Not recommended *i* +43 (0) 5572 232 32 0

Austria

Karawankentunnel (A11)

♀ St Jakob → Jesenice (Slovenia) ▲ 597 / 1959 / 1% 🗓 Normally open all year ⚲ Yes 🚐 May be used *i* www.asfinag.at/maut/sonder-und-videomaut

 Katschberg Pass (B99)

♀ St Michael in Lungau → Rennweg ▲ 1641 / 5384 / 17% 🗓 Normally open all year ⚲ No 🚐 Prohibited (must use Tauernautobahn)

 Kaunertal Gletscherstraße (L18)

♀ Prutz → Kaunertal ▲ 2750 / 9022 / 14% 🗓 Normally open all year ⚲ Yes 🚐 May be used *i* www.kaunertaler-gletscher.at/en/preise/gletscherstrasse

 Loibl (Ljubelj) Pass (B91)

♀ Ferlach → Kranj (Slovenia) ▲ 1369 / 4491 / 17% 🗓 Normally open all year ⚲ No 🚐 Prohibited *i* +43 (0) 463 325 23 0

 Malta-Hochalpenstraße

♀ Gmünd → Kölnbreinsperre ▲ 1930 / 6332 / 13% 🗓 Open May to Oct ⚲ Yes 🚐 Not recommended *i* www.kaerntencard.at/en/tourist-destinations/ausflugsziel-detail/malta-hochalmstrasse-95/

 Nassfeld (Pramollo) Pass (B90)

♀ Hermagor → Pontebba (Italy) ▲ 1552 / 5092 / 16% 🗓 Some closures Nov to Mar ⚲ No 🚐 Not recommended *i* +43 (0) 463 325 23 0

 Nockalmstraße

♀ Reichenau → Innerkrems ▲ 2040 / 6693 / 10% 🗓 Open May to Oct ⚲ Yes 🚐 Not recommended *i* www.nockalmstrasse.at/en/

 Ötztal Gletscherstraße (B186)

♀ Sölden → Tiefenbachferner ▲ 1927 / 6322 / 10% 🗓 Normally open all year ⚲ No 🚐 Not recommended *i* www.oetztal.com

 Pfaffensattel (L117)

♀ Rettenegg → Steinhaus am Semmering ▲ 1372 / 4501 / 16% 🗓 Normally open all year ⚲ Yes 🚐 Not recommended *i* +43 (0) 3853 300

 Plöcken (Monte Croce - Carnico) Pass (B110)

♀ Kötschach → Paluzza (Italy) ▲ 1357 / 4452 / 13% 🗓 Normally open all year ⚲ No 🚐 Not recommended *i* +43 (0) 463 325 23 0

 Pyhrnautobahn (A9)

♀ Bosruck → Gleinalm ▲ 817 / 2680 / 4% ⏱ Normally open all year ⚲ Yes 🚐 May be used *i* www.asfinag.at/maut/sonder-und-videomaut

Seeberg (Jezersko) Pass (B82)

📍 Bad Eisenkappel → Kranj (Slovenia) 🏔 1215 / 3986 / 12% 📅 Normally open all year
🔗 No 🚐 Not recommended *i* +43 (0) 463 325 23 0

 Silvretta Hochalpenstraße (P188/B188)

📍 Galtür → Partenen 🏔 2032 / 6667 / 14% 📅 Open June to mid-Nov 🔗 Yes 🚐 Prohibited
i en.silvretta-bielerhoehe.at/

 Tauernautobahn (A10)

📍 Flachau → Rennweg 🏔 1340 / 4396 / 5% 📅 Normally open all year 🔗 Yes 🚐 Alternative to
Katschberg Pass; may be used *i* www.asfinag.at/maut/sonder-und-videomaut

 Tauernschleuse (Motorail)

📍 Böckstein → Mallnitz 🏔 1226 / 4022 / NA 📅 Normally open all year 🔗 Yes 🚐 Special
conditions in summer for trailers *i* www.gasteinertal.com/autoschleuse

 Thurn Pass (B161)

📍 Kitzbühel → Mittersill 🏔 1273 / 4177 / 8% 📅 Normally open all year 🔗 No 🚐 May be used

 Timmelsjoch (Rombo) Pass (B186)

📍 Untergurgl → Timmelsjoch (Italian border) 🏔 2509 / 8232 / 13% 📅 Open June to mid-Oct
🔗 Yes 🚐 Prohibited towards Italy; not recommended towards Austria *i* www.timmelsjoch.com/
en/

 Turracher Höhe (B95)

📍 Predlitz → Reichenau 🏔 1783 / 5850 / 23% 📅 Normally open all year 🔗 No 🚐 Not
recommended

 Villacher Alpenstraße

📍 Möltschach → Dobratsch 🏔 1732 / 5682 / 9% 📅 Normally open all year 🔗 Yes 🚐 Not
recommended *i* www.villacher-alpenstrasse.at/en/

 Wurzen (Koren) Pass (B109)

📍 Villach → Kranjska Gora (Slovenia) 🏔 1073 / 3520 / 18% 📅 Normally open all year 🔗 No
🚐 Prohibited *i* +43 (0) 463 325 23 0

Zirler Berg (B177)

📍 Zirl → Seefeld 🏔 1057 / 3468 / 16% 📅 Normally open all year 🔗 No 🚐 Prohibited
northbound; not recommended southbound

Current traffic information is available from:

www.oeamtc.at/portal/berg-passstrassen+2500++500408

Belgium

For the visiting motorist, despite its beautiful historic cities, Belgium often gets a bad press. Its drivers have a poor reputation and many of its busy motorways are now in urgent need of repair. Its capital, Brussels, is often severely congested: avoid the centre during rush hour if you can. If you are travelling through the city, a network of tunnels carries much of the direct traffic, but these can be very confusing for strangers: take time in advance to familiarise yourself with your route and the exit you will need to take.

In 2015, Brussels introduced one of the largest pedestrianised areas in Europe, so – as with many of Belgium's cities – you may do better to park your car in one of the city's multi-storey car parks, or – usually for stays not exceeding two hours – in a Blue Zone parking area, where you'll need to display a parking disc. In other districts, you may find signs indicating that you should park fully or partly on the pavement.

Once you are moving again, trams always have priority. If you are stopped in traffic, you should switch off your engine to reduce pollution. In many old cities, you will still find the traditional cobblestones or 'pavé': take it easy on these, as they can be hard on your car's suspension and very slippery in the wet.

Narrow streets in the centre of Brussels, with dedicated parking for bicycles. (Courtesy mathess/Thinkstock)

Belgium's motorways are free, adding to the high level of traffic using them. To cope with this, Belgium has an unusual rule near some intersections, forbidding the use of cruise control, in case motorists fail to slow down in time for queuing traffic. The police can levy on-the-spot fines, and your car may be permanently confiscated if you fail to pay. As in France, motorcyclists may ride between lanes of slow-moving vehicles, but must not exceed 50km/h.

Traditional cobblestones in the historic city of Mons. (Courtesy J Jeanmart/Belgian Tourist Office)

Belgium

Parking partly on pavement, partly in road (left); No parking on pavement (middle); and Compulsory parking on pavement signs.

Traffic queues likely ahead

No entry, in either direction, for any vehicles

Motorway signs have green background

SPEED LIMITS

		km/h
🏠 Towns/villages	(50) / (20) or (30)	schools and residential zones
🅰 Main roads	(90) 🕇 Motorways	(120)

Use of cruise control prohibited until next intersection

End of restriction on use of cruise control

GENERAL RULES

Y	Drink-drive limit (g/l blood)	0.5 / 0.2 for novice drivers (first two years)
🧍	Children in front seats	Min 1.35m height, unless suitable restraint used
👪	Min driving age	18 / 21-23 to rent car
✳	Licence or IDP	✅ UK photocard or three-part pink licence recommended
🖪	Insurance: Green Card	✅ Recommended
☼	DRL	✅ Recommended
📱	Mobile phones	⊘ Handheld prohibited ✖ Hands-free tolerated, but not recommended
📶	Radar detectors	⊘ Prohibited
📷	GPS speed camera alerts (POI)	✅ Allowed
➕	Emergency services	Call 112
⚒	Special rules	• Priority to the right: give way to vehicles approaching from the right (unless signs indicate otherwise) • Filter in turn when two lanes of traffic merge • Use of dashcams not recommended

Tongeren 20

Main road signs have blue background

DRIVING EQUIPMENT

🅰	Warning triangle	◯	Required
👕	High-vis jacket(s)	◯	Required
🧰	First-aid kit	◯	Required for cars registered in Belgium; recommended for visitors
🧯	Fire extinguisher	◯	Required for cars registered in Belgium; recommended for visitors
💡	Spare bulbs	✅	Recommended
⛽	Spare fuel (can)	⚠	Prohibited on ferries, otherwise allowed
⚙	Winter tyres	✅	Recommended in wintry conditions
❄	Snow chains	✅	Allowed on snow or ice

TOLLS

🕇	Currently free, but vignette-based tolls are under discussion
⊙	Kil, Liefkenshoek & Westerschelde Tunnels

P&O's Pride of York heads up the River Humber into Hull. (Courtesy Andy Beecroft)

Travelling to and from Belgium

Since the closure of the service from Zeebrugge to Rosyth to passenger traffic at the end of 2010, there has been only one regular ferry crossing from Belgium to the UK. Although the ships are older than the flagship vessels on the Dover-Calais route, P&O's regular overnight crossing to Hull is a relaxed journey, with plenty of time to enjoy a drink and evening meal on board before turning in for the night. Traffic on the approach to the port at Zeebrugge can be slow, so allow plenty of time to check-in.

Port information

Ferry operator contacts

P&O Ferries   www.poferries.com   +32 28 08 50 20

KEY 🛳 Service operator
i Info ♀ Location 🖳 GPS
▉ Exit routes

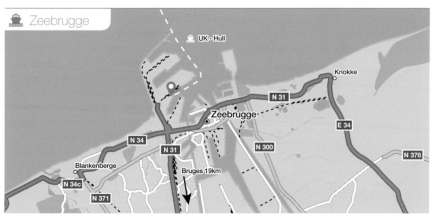

🛳 P&O Ferries: UK – Hull *i* www.portofzeebrugge.be ♀ Leopold II-dam 13, 8380 Zeebrugge
🖳 51.340 N, 3.187 E

France & Monaco

France is the world's most popular destination for tourists, and England's closest neighbour. With lots to see only a short drive from the Channel ports, it's a great place to start driving abroad. Despite some recent increases, accident rates have decreased markedly over the past decade. Speeds have fallen on main roads, with many speed cameras and on-the-spot fines of up to €375. For drivers exceeding the limit by 40km/h or more, the police may seize your licence, or even impound your car.

You may still find French drivers more aggressive than you're used to, though, especially in major cities. Typically, they flash their headlights to warn that they are coming through and not to give way. Attitudes to drinking and driving may seem more relaxed, but don't take any risks, as the limit is lower than in England & Wales, or many US states.

The most important rule to observe in France is the notorious 'priorité à droite:' in built-up areas and whenever you see the yellow diamond sign with a black bar through

The majestic sweep of the A41 autoroute, from Annecy to Geneva, in the French Alps. (Courtesy APRR/Véronique Paul)

it (page 62), you must give way to traffic approaching from the right. When entering a town or village, the place name sign indicates the start of a 50km/h speed limit. Local drivers often take a cavalier approach to parking scrapes, and fail to heed pedestrian crossings, so take care when stopping if cars are close behind you.

Clear blue background for the signs on all French autoroutes, here near Reims. (Courtesy Groupe SANEF/Alain Hatat)

Away from the cities, traffic is often light, although the summer months can be very busy. Check online at www.bison-fute. gouv.fr for the dates to avoid, or look for the 'Itinéraires bis' signs on main routes: these will divert you onto less crowded side roads.

France has an excellent, albeit expensive, network of toll motorways, with frequent rest areas. Traffic information is regularly broadcast on 107.7 FM, with some reports in English. Watch out for motorcyclists forcing their way between lanes of cars: officially, this is allowed in slow-moving queues, but is often

Special lane for 'Liber-t' badge holders at the 'péage' or toll booth. (Courtesy Vinci Autoroutes/ Jean-Philippe Moulet)

Entering a built-up area: 50km/h speed limit and priority to the right!

abused. You can get through the toll booths much faster with a 'Liber-t' tag, now available to non-residents (see checklist, page 62). If you break down, you must use the official contractor to be towed off the motorway before your own breakdown cover takes effect. In case of accident, both parties should complete a 'constat amiable,' the French version of the European Accident Statement Form.

Monaco

The same rules apply as in France, but caravans are not allowed to enter the Principality.

Numerous rest areas are a welcome feature of all French autoroutes. (Courtesy Groupe SANEF/Eric Bernard)

Ouch! Street parking, Paris-style.

France & Monaco

France & Monaco

Speed camera
ahead

Residential zone
(20km/h speed
limit)

Priorité à droite:
priority to the right

Motorway toll
lane for cars with
electronic tag

Give way

Ring road

Switch on lights

Fortnightly parking
on alternate sides

SPEED LIMITS   km/h

🏘 Towns/villages	**50**	
🛣 Main roads	**90** / **80**	new drivers + in wet
🛣 Motorways	**130** / **110**	new drivers + in wet

GENERAL RULES

Drink-drive limit (g/l blood)	0.5 / 0.2 for novice drivers (first three years)	
Children in front seats	Min 10 yo	
Min driving age	18 (21-25 to rent car)	
Licence or IDP	✓	UK photocard or three-part pink licence recommended
Insurance: Green Card	✓	Recommended
DRL	✓	Recommended
Mobile phones	⊘	Handhelds and earphones prohibited
	⚠	Hands-free with Bluetooth connection only
Radar detectors	⊘	Prohibited
GPS speed camera alerts (POI)	⊘	Prohibited
Emergency services	Call 112	
Special rules		

- Priority to the right: give way to vehicles approaching from the right (unless signs indicate otherwise)
  Give way to trams. Do not overtake stationary trams when passengers are alighting
  Access restrictions to Paris for vehicles causing pollution to be introduced during 2016
  No smoking with children under 12 in car
- Flip-flops may not be worn when driving

i uk.rendezvousenfrance.com/en/information/driving-france-0

DRIVING EQUIPMENT

A	Warning triangle	○	Required
🦺	High-vis jacket(s)	○	Required (inside vehicle)
🧰	First-aid kit	✓	Recommended
🧯	Fire extinguisher	✓	Recommended
💡	Spare bulbs	○	Required
⛽	Spare fuel (can)	⚠	Prohibited on ferries and Eurotunnel, otherwise allowed
❄	Winter tyres	✓	Recommended in wintry conditions
❄	Snow chains	✓	Chains or approved snow socks required according to conditions/as signed
📦	Additional items	○	Two single-use breathalysers (check expiry dates). Fines no longer levied, but still legally required

TOLLS

🛣	Tolls on most motorways outside major cities
💳	How to pay Cash / Credit Card / Tag (Liber-t)
i	www.autoroutes.fr www.saneftolling.co.uk
🔅	Tolls for some mountain tunnels: see page 66

One of Condor's ferries passes in front of the old city of Saint-Malo. (Courtesy Condor Ferries Ltd)

France & Monaco

Travelling to and from France

Boarding one of DFDS Seaways' ships on the Dover-Dunkirk route. (Courtesy DFDS Seaways)

For many British motorists, France will be their gateway to the Continent, as well as their favourite destination in its own right. There are nine ports to choose from, from Dunkirk, close to the Belgian border, to Calais, the busiest port of all, and Dieppe, which is the shortest distance from Paris. Further west, the ports of Caen-Ouistreham, Cherbourg, Le Havre, Roscoff and Saint-Malo are ideal for travellers to or from the beautiful regions of Normandy and Brittany, but also for motorists driving down to the Loire Valley or into south-west France.

Port information

Eurotunnel and ferry operator contacts:

Brittany Ferries	www.brittany-ferries.co.uk	+33 825 828 828
Condor Ferries	www.condorferries.co.uk	+33 825 135 135
DFDS Seaways	www.dfdsseaways.co.uk	See website for phone number for each route
Eurotunnel	www.eurotunnel.com/uk/home	+33 810 63 03 04
P&O Ferries	www.poferries.com	+33 3 66 74 03 25
Stena Line	www.stenaline.co.uk	+31 174 315 811

Caen-Ouistreham

KEY Service operator
i Info Location GPS
Exit routes

Brittany Ferries: UK – Portsmouth *i* www.brittany-ferries.co.uk/guides/ports/caen Avenue du Grand Large, 14150 Ouistreham 49.284 N, -0.250 W

Calais & Coquelles

DFDS Seaways: UK – Dover *i* www.calais-port.fr 54 rue du quai de la Loire, 62105 Calais 50.967 N, 1.870 E

P&O Ferries: UK – Dover *i* www.calais-port.fr 54 rue du quai de la Loire , 62105 Calais 50.967 N, 1.870 E

Eurotunnel: UK – Folkestone *i* www. eurotunnel.com/uk/home 62231 Coquelles 50.936 N, 1.815 E

Cherbourg

Brittany Ferries: UK – Poole & Portsmouth *i* www.brittany-ferries.co.uk/guides/ports/cherbourg Quai de Normandie, 50100 Cherbourg 49.645 N, -1.605 W

Stena Line: Ireland – Rosslare *i* www. stenaline.co.uk/routes/rosslare-cherbourg/Port-Cherbourg/ Quai de Normandie, 50100 Cherbourg 49.645 N, -1.605 W

France & Monaco

🚢 DFDS Seaways (will be re-branded from spring 2016): UK – Newhaven *i* www.portdedieppe.fr/ ♀ 7, Quai Gaston Lalitte, 76200 Dieppe 🖥 49.934 N, 1.090 E

🚢 DFDS Seaways: UK – Dover *i* www.dfdsseaways.co.uk/customer-service/port-information/ ♀ Terminal Roulier du Port Ouest, 59279 Loon-Plage 🖥 51.021 N, 2.198 E

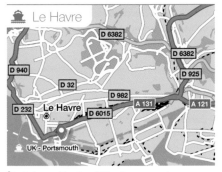

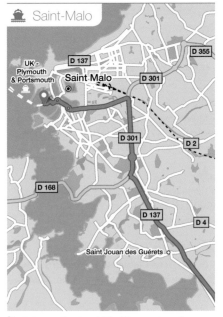

🚢 Brittany Ferries: UK – Portsmouth *i* www.brittany-ferries.co.uk/guides/ports/le-havre ♀ Terminal de la Citadelle, 76600 Le Havre 🖥 49.489 N, 0.120 E

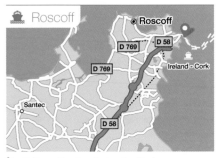

🚢 Brittany Ferries: Ireland – Cork *i* www.brittany-ferries.co.uk/guides/ports/roscoff ♀ Port du Bloscon, 29680 Roscoff 🖥 48.722 N, -3.967 W

🚢 Brittany Ferries: UK – Plymouth and Portsmouth *i* www.brittany-ferries.co.uk/guides/ports/st-malo ♀ Gare Maritime du Naye, 35400 Saint-Malo 🖥 48.643 N, -2.024 W

🚢 Condor Ferries: UK – Poole *i* www.condorferries.co.uk/destinations/stmalo-port.aspx ♀ Gare Maritime du Naye, 35400 Saint-Malo 🖥 48.642 N, -2.023 W

France & Monaco

Mountain roads and tunnels

Spring sunset over the Col de la Bonette. (Courtesy Andrew Mayovskyy/Thinkstock) / A steep gradient, sharp bends and snow poles for winter: caution advised.

KEY ♀ → Location ▲ Statistics: height m / ft / max gradient 🗓 When open � Toll 🚐 Caravans+trailers *i* Info

 Agnel (D205T)
♀ Molines en Queyras → Casteldelfino (Italy) ▲ 2746 / 9009 / 16% 🗓 Open Jun to mid-Oct � No 🚐 Not recommended

 Allos (D908)
♀ Barcelonnette → Colmars ▲ 2250 / 7382 / 9% 🗓 Open end May to Nov � No 🚐 Prohibited

 Aravis (D909)
♀ Flumet → La Clusaz ▲ 1486 / 4875 / 8% 🗓 Some closures Dec to Mar � No 🚐 May be used

 Ballon d'Alsace (D465)
♀ St Maurice-sur-Moselle → Giromagny ▲ 1171 / 3842 / 9% 🗓 Some closures Dec to Mar � No 🚐 May be used

 Bayard (N85)
♀ Chauvet → Brutinel ▲ 1248 / 4094 / 12% 🗓 Normally open all year � No 🚐 Not recommended

 Cayolle (D902)
♀ Barcelonnette → Guillaumes ▲ 2326 / 7631 / 11% 🗓 Open May to Nov � No 🚐 Prohibited

 Croix de Fer (D926)
♀ St Jean de Maurienne → Allemont ▲ 2086 / 6844 / 12% 🗓 Open Jun to Oct � No 🚐 Not recommended

 Croix-Haute (D1075)
♀ Monestier-de-Clermont → Aspres-sur-Buëch ▲ 1179 / 3868 / 9% 🗓 Normally open all year � No 🚐 May be used

 Croix-Morand (D996)
♀ Mont-Dore → Lac Chambon ▲ 1401 / 4596 / 8% 🗓 Normally open all year � No 🚐 Not recommended

 Faucille (N5)
♀ Gex → Morez ▲ 1320 / 4331 / 8% 🗓 Normally open all year � No 🚐 May be used

France & Monaco

Galibier (D902)

St Michel de Maurienne → Col du Lautaret 2645 / 8678 / 14% Open mid-June to Oct No Not recommended

 ### Glandon (D926/927)

La Chambre → Barrage de Verney 1951 / 6401 / 15% Open Jun to Oct No Not recommended

 ### Ibañeta/Roncesvalles

Arneguy → Burguete (Spain) 1057 / 3468 / 7% Normally open all year No May be used

 ### Iseran (D902)

Val d'Isère → Lanslebourg 2770 / 9088 / 12% Open mid-June to Oct No Not recommended

 ### Izoard (D902)

Briançon → Guillestre 2360 / 7743 / 12% Open Jun to Oct No Not recommended

 ### La Bonette/Restefond (SG3)

Jausiers → St Etienne de Tinée 2802 / 9193 / 12% Open mid-June to Oct No Not recommended

 ### Larche/Colle della Maddalena (D900)

La Condamine-Châtelard → Bagni di Vinadio (Italy) 1991 / 6532 / 8% Some closures Dec to Mar No May be used

Lautaret (D1091)

Briançon → Le Bourg d'Oisans 2058 / 6752 / 10% Some closures Dec to Mar No Not recommended

 ### Mont Blanc Tunnel (N205)

Chamonix → Courmayeur (Italy) 1381 / 4531 / NA Normally open all year Yes May be used *i* www.tunnelmb.net

 ### Mont Cenis (D1086)

Lanslebourg → Susa (Italy) 2083 / 6834 / 11% Open May to mid-Nov No Not recommended

 ### Mont Ventoux (D974)

Bédoin → Malaucène 1912 / 6273 / 11% Open mid-May to mid-Nov No Not recommended *i* www.bedoin.org

 ### Montgenèvre (SS24)

Briançon → Cesare Torinese (Italy) 1854 / 6083 / 12% Normally open all year No May be used

 ### Petit St Bernard (D1090/SS26)

Bourg St Maurice → Pré-Saint-Didier (Italy) 2188 / 7178 / 9% Open Jun to Oct No Not recommended

 ### Schlucht (D417)

Xonrupt-Longemer → Munster 1139 / 3737 / 7% Normally open all year No May be used

 ### Turini (D2565)

La Bollène-Vésubie → Sospel 1604 / 5262 / 9% Some closures Dec to Mar No Not recommended

 ### Vars (D902)

St Paul-sur-Ubaye → Guillestre 2109 / 6919 / 12% Some closures Dec to Mar No Not recommended

France & Monaco

Germany

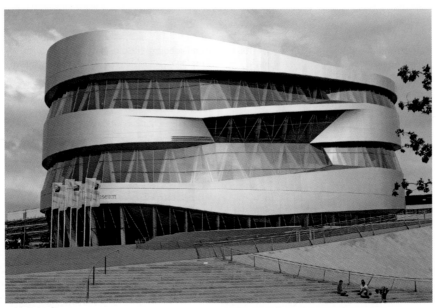

The Mercedes-Benz Museum, Stuttgart: a symbol of excellence in German automotive engineering.

Germany is famous as one of the last places in the world with no overall speed limit, a right still fiercely defended by its citizens. Its drivers are fast, but disciplined: when speed limits do apply, Germans usually respect them scrupulously, and there are high on-the-spot fines for offenders.

Germany has extensive restrictions on access to its city centres: to enter these 'Umweltzonen,' drivers must obtain an environmental sticker ('Umweltplakette'), with different colours for different levels of pollution. Most modern cars will qualify for a green (level four) sticker. The stickers are valid nationwide, and may be ordered online (see www.tolltickets.com), or from any DEKRA testing station in Germany. Exemptions may be obtained for historic cars. In towns, blue

A green 'Umweltplakette' allowing this car to enter the controlled city centres.

For more information scan the QR code or visit the Toll Tickets website at:

www.tolltickets.com

parking discs ('Parkscheiben') – available from newsagents and petrol stations – are widely used.

On the autobahn

Few driving experiences can match passing a de-restriction sign and speeding along an unlimited German motorway. But it's precisely

Road works and heavy traffic on the A3 autobahn near Würzburg. (Courtesy ADAC)

that exhilaration which drivers new to the autobahn should be wary of. Avoid the temptation to floor the throttle straight away, and build your speed gradually. Things happen fast when you're travelling at 100mph (160km/h) or more, so you need to anticipate the moves of other vehicles much further in advance. Scan the road far ahead, and watch out for trucks pulling out on two-lane sections of autobahn. Look much further behind in your rear-view mirror too: that speck in the distance might be a Porsche coming up at 150mph (nearly 250km/h)! After overtaking, get back into the right-hand lane as soon as possible.

If you don't feel comfortable driving at such speeds, remember you don't have to: it's fine to cruise at your usual safe speed. And you should always slow right down when it's wet or visibility is poor. Sometimes traffic will hold you up anyway: many routes are congested, with frequent roadworks. If traffic backs up, you must create a free lane between the lines of vehicles, so that emergency vehicles can get through. When two lanes of traffic merge into one, use the 'zipper' principle and filter in-turn.

Prolonged high-speed driving will put extra strain on your car, so check it carefully before starting off. Pay special attention to the condition of your tyres, and whether the manufacturer recommends higher pressures. You'll also get through fuel more quickly, and it's an offence to run out of fuel on the autobahn.

Emergency accident teams at work. (Courtesy ADAC) / A Jaguar XJ at speed on the autobahn near Frankfurt. (Courtesy supergenijalac/Thinkstock)

Germany

Street lights not on at night: use parking lights

Restriction when wet (eg lower speed limit)

Environmental zone

One-way street

SPEED LIMITS   km/h

🏠	Towns/villages (50)	🚗	Main roads (100)
🛣	M'ways	No limit unless signposted / (130) recommended	

GENERAL RULES

🍸	Drink-drive limit (g/l blood)	0.5 / 0.3 in hazardous conditions 0.0 for new drivers (under 21 & first two years)
🧍	Children in front seats	Min 12 yo and 1.5m height, unless suitable restraint used Airbag must be deactivated if child seat used
👪	Min driving age	18
✴	Licence or IDP	✅ UK photocard or three-part pink licence recommended
📇	Insurance: Green Card	✅ Recommended
⚙	DRL	✅ Recommended
📱	Mobile phones	⊘ Handhelds prohibited ✕ Hands-free tolerated, but not recommended
📶	Radar detectors	⊘ Prohibited
📷	GPS speed camera alerts (POI)	⊘ Prohibited
➕	Emergency services	Call 112 (Police also 110)
⚒	Special rules	

- Priority to the right: give way to vehicles approaching from the right (unless signs indicate otherwise)
- Do not overtake school bus as it approaches stop
- Use dipped headlights in tunnels
- Use of dashcams not recommended
- Switch-off engine when waiting at level crossings
- ALL accidents (even minor) must be reported to police

i www.adac.de/infotestrat/ratgeber-verkehr/verkehrszeichen/default.aspx

Tram or bus stop

End of speed restriction

Recommended route (diversion)

Cars with trailers allowed

DRIVING EQUIPMENT

⚠	Warning triangle	○ Required
🦺	High-vis jacket(s)	○ Required for cars registered in Germany; recommended for visitors
🧰	First-aid kit	○ Required for cars registered in Germany; recommended for visitors
🔥	Fire extinguisher	✅ Recommended
💡	Spare bulbs	✅ Recommended
⛽	Spare fuel (can)	⚠ Prohibited on ferries, otherwise allowed
⚙	Winter tyres	○ Winter tyres mandatory in wintry conditions (fines for delays or accidents caused by vehicles with unsuitable equipment)
❄	Snow chains	✅ Snow socks may be used in place of chains when required, max 50km/h

TOLLS

🛣		New toll for all roads planned for 2016 (motorways only for foreign-registered vehicles)
🚙	How to pay	Vignette (sticker) available for ten days/two months/full year
i		Check with motoring organisations
🅿		Herren & Warnow Tunnels Controlled access to many city centres (see main text)

Ireland

This section refers to the Republic of Ireland; for Northern Ireland, see the United Kingdom (page 82).

If you're reading this section as a British motorist, Ireland is an easy first step to driving abroad. Ireland attracts three million British visitors every year, drawn to beautiful scenic routes such as the Wild Atlantic Way. Driving – on the left – is very similar to what you'll experience in the UK. Outside the major cities, traffic is light, and drivers are generally relaxed and courteous, making for a largely stress-free trip, and one of the lowest accident rates in Europe. The biggest difference – for British and American visitors – is that Ireland has used kilometres, not miles, for speed limits and distance signs since 2005. English and Irish are both official languages, and most road signs are bilingual. In some areas (known as 'Gaeltacht'), where Irish predominates, you may see signs in Irish only.

40% of Ireland's population of 4.3 million lives within 100km (62 miles) of Dublin. Despite recent improvements to the road network, including the M50 West Link Motorway and the Dublin Port Tunnel, traffic in the capital is often very heavy, and the city should be avoided at rush hour if possible. Parking charges vary by zone, and the creation of a new tramway system (the 'Luas') makes it easier to come in by public transport.

Away from the major cities, public transport is less extensive, so a car is essential to get around. The network of motorways (numbered 'M') has been gradually extended, albeit with toll charges for many major routes, cutting journey times. Minor roads, many of them narrow, are more variable in quality, and average speeds are low. Watch out, too, for farm animals, especially sheep, and for slippery roads in the wet, as rain is frequent.

Remembering to keep left can be hard when the roads are this empty. (Courtesy Tourism Ireland)

Sheep can be a hazard in rural areas. (Courtesy Tourism Ireland)

Ireland

71

Ireland

*Many country roads are single track only.
(Courtesy Tourism Ireland)*

Give way

Roundabout ahead | *Mini-roundabout ahead*

No parking

Pedestrianised street

Level crossing without warning lights ahead

Sheep on road

SPEED LIMITS   km/h

	Towns/villages	**50** / **30**	Dublin city centre
A	Main roads	**80** / **100**	
	Motorways	**120**	

GENERAL RULES

⟡	Drink-drive limit (g/l blood)	0.5 / 0.2 for new drivers (first two years)
⚹	Children in front seats	Min 3 yo, 1.5m height, 36kg, unless suitable restraint used
⚏	Min driving age	17 / 23 to rent car
✹	Licence or IDP	✓ UK photocard or three-part pink licence recommended
▭	Insurance: Green Card	✓ Recommended
✶	DRL	✓ Recommended
▯	Mobile phones	⊘ Handhelds prohibited ⊗ Hands-free tolerated, but not recommended
📶	Radar detectors	⊘ Prohibited
📷	GPS speed camera alerts (POI)	⊘ Prohibited
✚	Emergency services	Call 112 or 999
⚓	Special rules	• Drive on the left
i	www.ireland.com/en-gb/about-ireland/travelling-within-ireland/ www.rulesoftheroad.ie/rules-of-the-road-eng.pdf	

DRIVING EQUIPMENT

⚠	Warning triangle	✓ Recommended
⛤	High-vis jacket(s)	✓ Recommended
🧰	First-aid kit	✓ Recommended
⚱	Fire extinguisher	✓ Recommended
☖	Spare bulbs	✓ Recommended
⛽	Spare fuel (can)	⚠ Prohibited on ferries, otherwise allowed
✿	Winter tyres	❶ Rarely needed
❄	Snow chains	⊘ Prohibited

TOLLS

🛣	Tolls on certain motorways	
▭	How to pay	Cash or tag. M50 Dublin: Payzone outlets or phone (1890 50 10 50)
i	www.tii.ie/roads-tolling/tolling-information/	
◉	Dublin Port Tunnel: see link above	

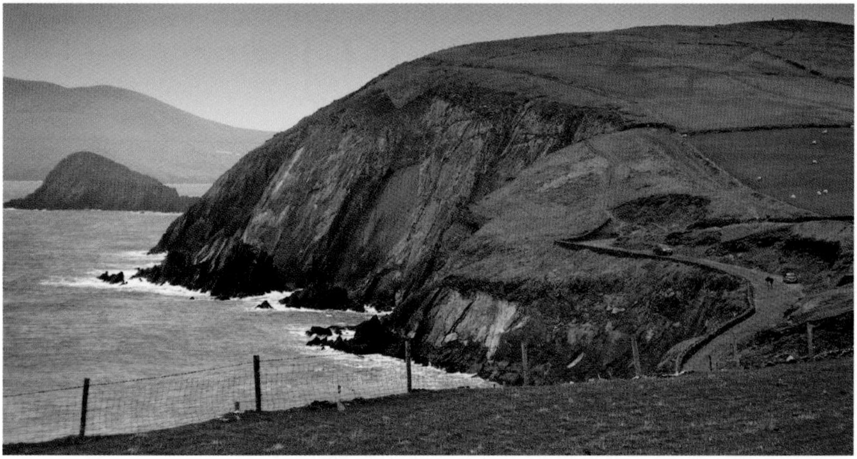

The Wild Atlantic Way, on the Irish coast. (Courtesy Tourism Ireland)

Travelling to and from Ireland

If you're heading to France from Ireland, the direct crossings from Cork and Rosslare make for a much more relaxing start to your holiday than crossing to the UK, and driving down through England to join one of the Channel ferries. Both routes offer overnight sailings, with comfortable cabins and full restaurant and bar service. Be warned, however, that these can be rough crossings if the weather is bad.

For crossings between the UK and Ireland, there are plenty of options: from Rosslare to Fishguard in South Wales, or from Dublin and nearby Dún Laoghaire to Holyhead, in North Wales. You can also cross from Belfast in Northern Ireland to Liverpool, or – in just over two hours – to Cairnryan in Scotland.

Port information

Ferry operator contacts

Brittany Ferries	www.brittany-ferries.co.uk	+353 21 4277 801
Stena Line	www.stenaline.co.uk	+353 1 204 7777

KEY Service operator
Info Location GPS
Exit routes

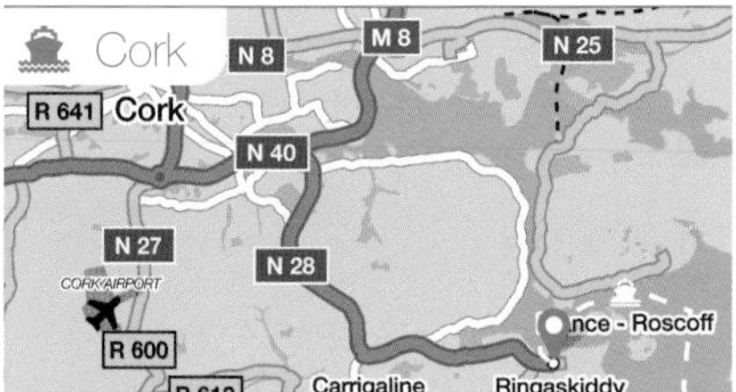

Brittany Ferries: France – Roscoff
i www.brittany-ferries.co.uk/guides/ports/cork
Ringaskiddy, Co Cork 51.831 N, -8.323 W

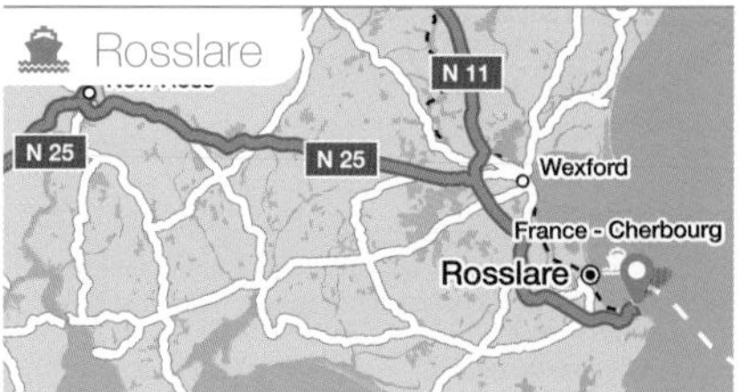

Stena Line: France – Cherbourg
i rosslareeuroport.irishrail.ie/home Europort, Rosslare, Co Wexford 52.251 N, -6.336 W

Luxembourg

uxembourg may often be just a brief stop en route elsewhere, but it has its own specific rules, and the police can issue on-the-spot fines for many offences. In towns, you should only sound your horn in immediate danger. A yellow line at the edge of the road indicates 'No parking', and if you park your car at night in an area without street lighting, you must leave your sidelights on.

For fans of mobile technology, the use of dashcams is not recommended, due to concerns about data privacy. Removable satnav devices should be positioned near the bottom corner of the windscreen, so that they do not block the driver's view. And if you have an MP3 or other music player, it's an offence to use it with headphones whilst driving.

SPEED LIMITS — km/h

Towns/villages	**50** / **20**	residential areas
Main roads	**90**	
Motorways	**130** / **110**	in wet weather

GENERAL RULES

Drink-drive limit (g/l blood)	0.5 / 0.2 for new drivers (first two years)	
Children in front seats	Min 12 yo, 1.5m height, 36kg, unless suitable restraint used	
Min driving age	18	
Licence or IDP	✓	UK photocard or three-part pink licence recommended
Insurance: Green Card	✓	Recommended
DRL	✓	Recommended
Mobile phones	⊘	Handhelds prohibited
	✗	Hands-free tolerated, but not recommended
Radar detectors	⊘	Prohibited
GPS speed camera alerts (POI)	✓	Allowed
Emergency services		Call 112 (Police also 113)

Special rules
- Filter in turn when two lanes of traffic merge
- Switch off hazard warning lights when stopped at end of queue of cars
- Flash headlights at night when overtaking outside built-up areas
- In tunnels, use dipped headlights and keep 5m distance even when stopped

i www.visitluxembourg.com/en/travelguide/ transport-to-luxembourg/

Merge in turn ('système tirette')

Reduced visibility

Alternate side parking (by day of month)

School crossing

DRIVING EQUIPMENT

⚠	Warning triangle	○	Required
🦺	High-vis jacket(s)	○	Required for all passengers Also by pedestrians on unlit roads at night
🧰	First-aid kit	✓	Recommended
🧯	Fire extinguisher	✓	Recommended
💡	Spare bulbs	✓	Recommended
⛽	Spare fuel (can)	⊘	Prohibited
⚙	Winter tyres	○	Winter tyres on all wheels required in wintry conditions
❄	Snow chains	✓	Allowed on snow or ice
🧴	Additional items	○	Ensure you have sufficient fuel in tank

TOLLS

🛣	M'ways free	🚫	No other tolls

The Netherlands

There has been a regular boat crossing from the UK to the Netherlands since the late 19th century, and today it's easy to get around, whether you are travelling within the country or continuing to Germany and beyond. Driving conditions are generally excellent: the Netherlands has an extensive, free motorway network and an enviable safety record. Fines for speeding are some of the highest in Europe, and the Dutch usually respect speed limits: these have been marked on the road surface since 2015, although if a lower speed limit is signposted, that should be adhered to.

The Netherlands has no fewer than 12 million bicycles, for a population of 15 million, so local drivers are used to sharing the road with cycles (and skateboards too). Take care as a visitor: cyclists are always vulnerable and, surprisingly, cycle helmets are not a legal requirement. Watch out for the special bike lanes and dedicated traffic signals in towns. At junctions, give way when there is a row of white triangular signs on the road, and never cross a solid white line, even if turning off a road. A yellow and white diamond-shaped sign (see page 76) indicates that you have the right of way. Horns should not be used at all at night, and sparingly by day.

Watch out for carefree cyclists everywhere! (Courtesy NBTC Holland Marketing)

Distinctive yellow livery of emergency ambulances. (Courtesy lampixels/Thinkstock)

Modern IJburg Bridge. (Courtesy Herman Brinkman/Freeimages.com)

Large cities like Amsterdam are zoned into numbered districts, and it will help you find your way if you know the district for your destination. Parking discs are widely used, but 'Stopverband' means no parking or stopping. At night, leave your sidelights on if you park more than 30m (100ft) from a streetlamp. Some car parks have specific places for vehicles powered by LPG, which is widely available. 'Blue One 95' petrol, with a 15% ethanol content, is also being introduced, but may not be suitable for all cars.

Right of way (on priority road)

Hard shoulder open (as rush hour lane)

District numbers

Cycle path

Reduced visibility

Retractable bollard

SPEED LIMITS

		km/h
🏠 Towns/villages	**50** / **10** in Home Zones	
🅰 Main roads	**80**	
🚏 Motorways	**130**	

GENERAL RULES

🍷 Drink-drive limit (g/l blood)	0.5 / 0.2 for new drivers (first five years)	
👶 Children in front seats	Min 12 yo, 1.35m height, unless suitable restraint used	
👥 Min driving age	18	
✳ Licence or IDP	✔	UK photocard or three-part pink licence recommended
📖 Insurance: Green Card	✔	Recommended
⭕ DRL	✔	Recommended
📱 Mobile phones	⊘ Handhelds prohibited	
	✖ Hands-free tolerated, but not recommended	
📶 Radar detectors	⊘ Prohibited	
📷 GPS speed camera alerts (POI)	⊘ Prohibited	
➕ Emergency services	Call 112	
🔧 Special rules		

- Forbidden to cut across military convoys or funeral processions
- Trams and cycles have priority

ℹ https://goo.gl/NBMDLr

DRIVING EQUIPMENT

⚠ Warning triangle		⭕ Required	
📛 High-vis jacket(s)		✔ Recommended	
🧰 First-aid kit		✔ Recommended	
🧯 Fire extinguisher		✔ Recommended	
💡 Spare bulbs		✔ Recommended	
⛽ Spare fuel (can)		⚠ Prohibited on ferries, otherwise allowed	
⚙ Winter tyres		⚠ Spiked tyres prohibited	
❄ Snow chains		✔ Use according to conditions	

TOLLS

🚏 Free	
🔘	Westerscheldetunnel & Dordse Kil Tunnel

The Netherlands

Travelling to and from the Netherlands

The crossings to the Netherlands are ideal if you are heading to or from Germany, Poland or Scandinavia, especially since the closure of the direct route to Esbjerg in Denmark. The service to the Hook of Holland began as a crossing for train passengers in 1893, or you can cross to Rotterdam's Europoort or IJmuiden, just outside Amsterdam.

Port information

Ferry operator contacts

DFDS Seaways

www.dfdsseaways.co.uk   +31 255 54 6666

P&O Ferries

www.poferries.com   +31 10 714 54 64

Stena Line

www.stenaline.co.uk   +31 174 315 811

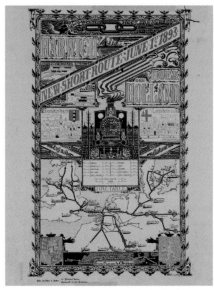

The crossing to the Hook of Holland dates back to 1893.

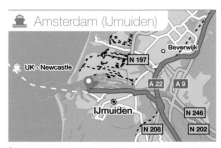

DFDS Seaways: UK – Newcastle *i* www. dfdsseaways.co.uk/customer-service/ port-information/ ♀ Sluisplein 33, 1975 AG Ijmuiden ⊡ 52.462 N, 4.587 E

KEY Service operator *i* Info ♀ Location
⊡ GPS ▬ Exit routes

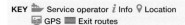

Stena Line: UK – Harwich ♀ Stationsweg 10, 3151 HS Hoek van Holland ⊡ 51.976 N, 4.126 E

P&O Ferries: UK – Hull ♀ Luxembourg Weg No.2, 3198 LG Europoort ⊡ 51.944 N, 4.132 E

Switzerland
& Liechtenstein

Mountains cover 70% of the country's area, and Switzerland has some of the world's most beautiful mountain roads. Its safety record is excellent, but take care on the steep mountain passes, with their frequent hairpin bends (see page 80). The distinctive yellow postal buses – part of Switzerland's extensive public transport system – have priority.

To use Switzerland's motorways, you'll need to buy an annual toll sticker ('Vignette'), valid from 1 December of the previous year, until 31 January the year following that shown. An additional 'Vignette' is required for caravans or other trailers. Swiss motorway signs have a green background, and main roads blue, which can be confusing,

The annual 'Vignette' (toll sticker) to use motorways in Switzerland.

as this is the opposite of France! If traffic backs-up on dual carriageway roads, you must create a free lane between the lines of vehicles, for emergency services to use. Vehicles on tow are limited to 40km/h and must leave the motorway at the next exit.

The Swiss are keen to protect the environment, and it's obligatory to switch off your engine at traffic lights or when stopped. Motorsport is mostly banned, and speeding is frowned upon, with stringent fines for offenders. If you are involved in a minor accident and decide not to call the police, it's compulsory to complete a European Accident Statement Form.

In built-up areas, yellow crosses at the edge of the road indicate that parking is prohibited. Parking discs – available from kiosks and petrol stations – are widely used in designated blue parking zones. When turning left at junctions, you must turn in front of the car turning left in the opposite lane. Finally, take special care when pedestrians are crossing the road: they will expect you to stop!

Distinctive yellow livery of one of Switzerland's postal buses. (Courtesy swiss-images.ch/Die Post)

Liechtenstein

Rules are closely aligned with those in Switzerland, but fines are higher. There are no motorway tolls.

Cars waiting to board the Vereina Motorail in winter. (Courtesy swiss-images.ch/ Rhaetische Bahn/Andrea Badrutt)

Postal route in mountains

500 m

Tunnel entrance in 500m

Zürich

Signs to main road have blue background

Basel

Signs to motorway have green background

Motorway (may be single carriageway)

One-way street with two-way cycle lane

Parking disc compulsory

Level crossing (with single flashing light)

Risk of gunshot noise

Switzerland & Liechtenstein

SPEED LIMITS
km/h

Towns/villages	**50**	
Main roads	**80** / **100**	
Motorways	**120**	

GENERAL RULES

Drink-drive limit (g/l blood)	0.5 / 0.1 for new drivers (first three years)	
Children in front seats	Min 12 yo and 1.5m height, unless suitable restraint used	
Min driving age	18	
Licence or IDP	✓	UK photocard or three-part pink licence recommended
Insurance: Green Card	✓	Recommended
DRL	O	Required for all cars registered after 1/1/1970
Mobile phones	⊘	Handhelds prohibited
	✗	Hands-free tolerated, but not recommended
Radar detectors	⊘	Prohibited
GPS speed camera alerts (POI)	⊘	Prohibited
Emergency services	Call 112	
TCS breakdown service	0800 140 140	
Special rules		

- Trams, postal vehicles, buses have priority
- Switch off engine at traffic lights or when stopped
- Use of dashcams not recommended

DRIVING EQUIPMENT

Warning triangle	O	Required
High-vis jacket(s)	✓	Recommended
First-aid kit	✓	Recommended
Fire extinguisher	✓	Recommended
Spare bulbs	✓	Recommended
Spare fuel (can)	✓	Permitted (max 25L)
Winter tyres	✓	Recommended Nov-Mar. Fines for delays or accidents caused by vehicles with unsuitable equipment Studded tyres allowed where appropriate from 24 Oct to 30 Apr, with 80km/h sticker at rear; prohibited on motorways
Snow chains	✓	Use according to conditions/when signed
Additional items	O	Spare glasses or contact lenses, if worn

TOLLS

Annual toll to use network	Additional vignette required for caravan/trailer
How to pay	Buy vignette at border, from petrol stations, or in advance from motoring organisations or link above
i	rail.myswitzerland.com/vignette.html

Mountain roads and tunnels

At the top of the Albula Pass. (Courtesy Swiss-image.ch/ Andy Mettler)

KEY ♀→ Location 📷 Statistics: height m / ft / max gradient 📅 When open 🏷 Toll 🚐 Caravans+trailers *i* Info

 Albula/Alvra Pass
♀ Bergün → La Punt 📷 2,312 / 7,585 / 12% 📅 Open late May to Oct 🏷 No 🚐 Not recommended

 Bernina Pass (29)
♀ Pontresina → Poschiavo 📷 2,328 / 7,638 / 12% 📅 Normally open all year 🏷 No 🚐 Not recommended; prohibited without special authorisation mid-Nov to mid-Apr

 Col de la Croix
♀ Villars-sur-Ollon → Les Diablerets 📷 1,776 / 5,827 / 12% 📅 Open May to Nov 🏷 No 🚐 Not recommended

 Flüela Pass (28)
♀ Davos → Susch 📷 2,383 / 7,818 / 11% 📅 Open May to early Dec 🏷 No 🚐 Not recommended; prohibited without special authorisation mid-Nov to mid-Apr

 Col de la Forclaz/des Montets
♀ Martigny → Argentière (France) 📷 1527 / 5010 / 8% 📅 Normally open all year 🏷 No 🚐 Not recommended

 Furka Pass (19) & Motorail
♀ Andermatt → Brig 📷 2436 / 7992 / 11% 📅 Pass open Jun to Oct; Motorail open all year 🏷 Yes (Motorail) 🚐 Prohibited (pass) *i* www.matterhorngotthardbahn.ch/en/Pages/default.aspx

 Grand St Bernard Pass (21) & Tunnel
♀ Martigny → Aosta (Italy) 📷 2473 / 8114 / 11% 📅 Open May/Jun to Oct 🏷 Yes (Tunnel) 🚐 Not recommended (pass) *i* www.letunnel.com

 Grimsel Pass (6)
♀ Innertkirchen → Gletsch 📷 2165 / 7103 / 11% 📅 Open May/Jun to Oct 🏷 No 🚐 Not recommended

 Jaun Pass
♀ Reidenbach → Broc 📷 1509 / 4951 / 14% 📅 Normally open all year 🏷 No 🚐 Not recommended

 Julier/Guglia Pass (3)
♀ Silvaplana → Tiefencastel 📷 2284 / 7493 / 13% 📅 Normally open all year 🏷 No 🚐 Not recommended; prohibited without special authorisation mid-Nov to mid-Apr

 Klausen Pass (17)
♀ Altdorf → Linthal 📷 1948 / 6391 / 10% 📅 Open late May to Oct 🏷 No 🚐 Prohibited

 Lenzerheide Pass (3)
♀ Chur → Tiefencastel 📷 1547 / 5075 / 11% 📅 Normally open all year 🏷 No 🚐 May be used

Forcola di Livigno (301)
📍 La Rosa → Livigno (Italy) 🏔 2315 / 7595 / 12% 📅 Open Jun to Nov 🚲 No 🚐 Not recommended; alternative Munt la Schera tunnel (toll)

 Lukmanier Pass (Lucomagno)
📍 Disentis → Acquarossa 🏔 1914 / 6280 / 10% 📅 Normally open all year 🚲 No 🚐 Not recommended

 Maloja Pass (3)
📍 Silvaplana → Chiavenna (Italy) 🏔 1815 / 5955 / 12% 📅 Normally open all year 🚲 No 🚐 Not recommended

 Nufenen (Novena) Pass
📍 Ulrichen → Airolo 🏔 2478 / 8130 / 13% 📅 Open Jun to Oct 🚲 No 🚐 Not recommended

 Oberalp/Orsera Pass (19) & Motorail
📍 Andermatt → Disentis 🏔 2044 / 6706 / 10% 📅 Open May to Oct; Motorail operates during winter closure 🚲 Yes (Motorail) 🚐 Not recommended (pass) ℹ www.matterhorngotthardbahn.ch/en/Pages/default.aspx

 Ofen/Fuorn Pass (28)
📍 Zernez → Santa Maria 🏔 2149 / 7051 / 12% 📅 Normally open all year 🚲 No 🚐 Not recommended

 Col du Pillon
📍 Aigle → Gstaad 🏔 1546 / 5072 / 11% 📅 Some closures Jan to Feb 🚲 No 🚐 Not recommended

 San Bernardino Pass (13) & Tunnel (A13)
📍 Hinterrhein → San Bernardino 🏔 2065 / 6775 / 12% 📅 Pass open May to Oct; tunnel open all year 🚲 Yes (A13 Tunnel) 🚐 Not recommended (pass): should use A13 Tunnel

 Simplon Pass (9)
📍 Brig → Iselle (Italy) 🏔 2005 / 6578 / 10% 📅 Normally open all year 🚲 No 🚐 Not recommended; Motorail available as alternative ℹ www.sbb.ch/en/station-services/car-bike/car-trains/autoverlad-simplon.html

 Splügen Pass (36)
📍 Splügen → Chiavenna (Italy) 🏔 2118 / 6949 / 13% 📅 Open May to Oct 🚲 No 🚐 Prohibited

 St Gotthard Pass (2) & Tunnel (A2)
📍 Airolo → Andermatt 🏔 2108 / 6916 / 10% 📅 Pass open Jun to Nov; tunnel open all year 🚲 Yes (A2 Tunnel) 🚐 Not recommended (pass): should use A2 Tunnel ℹ twitter.com/tcsgotthard

 Susten Pass (11)
📍 Innertkirchen → Wasser 🏔 2244 / 7362 / 9% 📅 Open Jun to Oct 🚲 No 🚐 Not recommended

 Umbrail Pass (38)
📍 Santa Maria im Münstertal → Bormio (Italy) 🏔 2501 / 8205 / 12% 📅 Open late May to Oct 🚲 No 🚐 Prohibited

 Wolfgang Pass (28)
📍 Davos → Klosters 🏔 1631 / 5351 / 10% 📅 Normally open all year 🚲 No 🚐 May be used

Current traffic information is available from:
www.oeamtc.at/portal/berg-passstrassen+2500++500408

United Kingdom

This section of the guide is, above all, designed to help visitors from outside the UK. But if you're reading this as a British motorist, you may find it interesting to see how your home country compares. The good news is that it does so very well: the UK has the second lowest fatal accident rate in Europe, and its motorists have a reputation for being courteous. Despite the challenge of driving on the left (for North American and other European visitors), it's a good place to begin driving in Europe. Around the major cities, traffic is often congested, but there are

The essence of England: vintage Lagonda at Chatsworth. (Courtesy VisitBritain)

many uncrowded roads in areas such as North Wales or the Scottish Highlands. The Isle of Man – which still has no speed limit outside built-up areas – is a mecca for motorcyclists.

Traffic is managed with a large number of roundabouts ('traffic circles' in US English) and so-called 'yellow box' junctions, which are covered with criss-cross yellow lines: motorists may only enter the box when their exit is clear. Yellow and red lines along the edge of the road show where you can't park (yellow lines) and where you can't park or stop (red lines). Single yellow or red lines cover restrictions at certain times (which are signposted); double lines indicate that you cannot park (yellow lines) or stop (red lines) at any time.

The TT race makes the Isle of Man a favourite with bikers. / Peaceful country roads in Lancashire, northern England. (Both Courtesy VisitBritain)

Scotland

Scotland has a lower drink-drive limit than the rest of the UK (see Checklist). Serious speeding offences are treated automatically as dangerous driving, and bans of a year or more imposed.

The Channel Islands

Cars are banned on Sark and Herm, and caravans and camper vans are admitted only with special advance permits on Jersey, Guernsey and Alderney. There is an overall speed limit of 40mph (64km/h) and the roads are packed in summer.

URBAN CLEARWAY
Monday to Friday

am	pm
8.00 - 9.30	4.30 - 6.30

No stopping during times shown except to set down or pick up passengers

Roundabout (give way to vehicles already on roundabout)

National speed limit applies (on leaving built-up area)

Road marking for the London Congestion Charge. (Courtesy ÖAMTC)

Audible warning of height limit at railway crossings

Elderly people present

Traffic lights not in use

Migratory toad crossing

Speed camera ahead

SPEED LIMITS

Note: speeds are mph

🏘 Towns/villages	**30**	(48km/h)	
A Main roads	**60**	(96km/h)	No limit on the Isle of Man
🏎 Motorways	**70**	(112km/h)	

GENERAL RULES

🍷	Drink-drive limit (g/l blood)	England & Wales: 0.8 Scotland: 0.5
🚸	Children in front seats	Min 12 yo and 1.35m height, unless suitable restraint used
👥	Min driving age	17 (car rental companies may require higher age)
✱	Licence or IDP	✅ National licence for EU citizens; IDP recommended for others
📇	Insurance: Green Card	✅ Recommended
☼	DRL	◯ Use in poor visibility
📱	Mobile phones	⊘ Handhelds prohibited / ✖ Hands-free tolerated, but not recommended
📶	Radar detectors	✅ Allowed
📟	GPS speed camera alerts (POI)	✅ Allowed
✚	Emergency services	Call 112 or 999
⚓	Special rules	• Drive on the left • No smoking with children under 18 in car
i	www.visitbritain.com/en/Transport/Getting-around-Britain/Driving-regulations-in-Britain.htm	

DRIVING EQUIPMENT

A	Warning triangle	◯	Required
🦺	High-vis jacket(s)	✅	Recommended
🩹	First-aid kit	✅	Recommended
🧯	Fire extinguisher	✅	Recommended
💡	Spare bulbs	✅	Recommended
⛽	Spare fuel (can)	⚠	Prohibited on ferries and Eurotunnel, otherwise allowed
⚙	Winter tyres	✅	Use according to conditions
❄	Snow chains		
🧳	Additional items	◯	Nationality sticker

TOLLS

🏎	Generally free, except M6 Toll motorway and some estuary crossings (eg Dartford Crossing, Humber Bridge, Severn Bridge)
💳	How to pay Cash/credit card
i	www.m6toll.co.uk
🔲	Central London: London Congestion Charge (Mon-Fri 0700-1800)
💳	How to pay Online/SMS/phone
i	www.tfl.gov.uk/modes/driving/congestion-charge

United Kingdom

Travelling to and from the United Kingdom

For many visitors to England, arriving by ferry will be synonymous with the white cliffs of Dover. But Dover's Eastern Docks, and the nearby Eurotunnel terminal in Folkestone, are only two of the many options for travellers to and from the UK. The Hindhead Tunnel, on the A3, has speeded the journey from London to Portsmouth, with frequent sailings across the Western Channel to Normandy, Brittany and Spain. For crossings to Belgium and the Netherlands, there are regular services from Harwich, Hull and Newcastle, which are a shorter drive from northern England or Scotland.

Port information

Eurotunnel and ferry operator contacts

Brittany Ferries	www.brittany-ferries.co.uk	+44 871 244 0744
Condor Ferries	www.condorferries.co.uk	+44 1202 207 216
DFDS Seaways	www.dfdsseaways.co.uk	See website for number for each route
Eurotunnel	www.eurotunnel.com/uk/home	+44 8443 35 35 35
P&O Ferries	www.poferries.com	+44 8716 64 64 64
Stena Line	www.stenaline.co.uk	+44 8447 70 70 70

KEY Service operator *i* Info ♀ Location 💻 GPS ▬ Exit routes

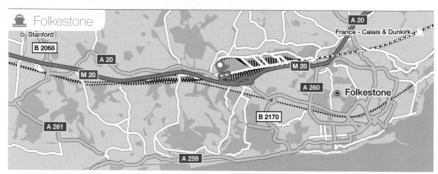

Dover

DFDS Seaways: France – Calais & Dunkirk *i* www.doverport.co.uk/ferry ♀ Eastern Docks, Dover CT16 1JA 💻 51.126 N, 1.327 E

P&O Ferries: France – Calais *i* www.doverport.co.uk/ferry ♀ Eastern Docks, Dover CT16 1JA 💻 51.126 N, 1.327 E

Folkestone

Eurotunnel: France – Calais (Coquelles) *i* www.eurotunnel.com/uk/home ♀ Ashford Road, Folkestone, CT18 8XX 💻 51.093 N, 1.119 E

⚓ Harwich

🚢 Stena Line: Netherlands – Hook of Holland
i www.stenaline.co.uk/routes/harwich-hook-of-holland/Port-Info ♀ Parkeston Quay, Parkeston, Harwich CO12 4SR 🖥 51.945 N, 1.252 E

⚓ Hull

🚢 P&O Ferries: Belgium – Zeebrugge
i www.abports.co.uk/Our_Locations ♀ King George Dock, Hedon Road, Hull HU9 5PR 🖥 53.744 N, -0.275 W

🚢 P&O Ferries: Netherlands – Rotterdam
i www.abports.co.uk/Our_Locations ♀ King George Dock, Hedon Road, Hull HU9 5PR 🖥 53.744 N, -0.275 W

⚓ Newcastle

🚢 DFDS Seaways: Netherlands – Amsterdam (IJmuiden) *i* www.dfdsseaways.co.uk/customer-service/port-information ♀ International Passenger Terminal, Royal Quays, North Shields NE29 6EE 🖥 54.993 N, -1.452 W

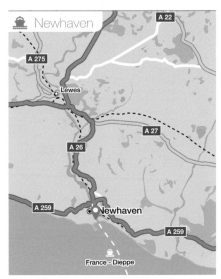

⚓ Newhaven

🚢 DFDS Seaways (will be re-branded from spring 2016): France – Dieppe *i* www.newhavenferryport.co.uk ♀ Railway Approach, Newhaven BN9 0DF 🖥 50.793 N, 0.054 W

United Kingdom

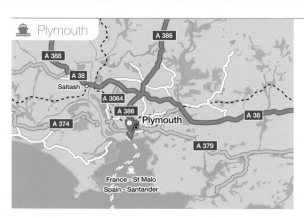

🚢 Plymouth

🛳 Brittany Ferries: France – St Malo *i* www.brittany-ferries.co.uk/guides/ports/plymouth ♀ Millbay, Plymouth PL1 1EW 📷 50.367 N, -4.156 W

🛳 Brittany Ferries: Spain – Santander *i* www.brittany-ferries.co.uk/guides/ports/plymouth ♀ Millbay, Plymouth PL1 1EW 📷 50.367 N, -4.156 W

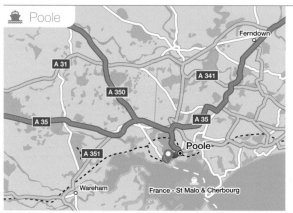

🚢 Poole

🛳 Brittany Ferries: France – Cherbourg *i* www.brittany-ferries.co.uk/guides/ports/poole ♀ New Harbour Road, Hamworthy, Poole BH15 4AJ 📷 50.709 N, -1.993 W

🛳 Condor Ferries: France – St Malo *i* www.condorferries.co.uk/destinations/poole-port.aspx ♀ New Harbour Road, Hamworthy, Poole BH15 4AJ 📷 50.709 N, -1.993 W

🚢 Portsmouth

🛳 Brittany Ferries: France – Caen, Cherbourg, Le Havre & St Malo *i* www.brittany-ferries.co.uk/guides/ports/portsmouth ♀ Wharf Road, Portsmouth PO2 8RU 📷 50.812 N, -1.087 W

🛳 Brittany Ferries: Spain – Bilbao & Santander *i* www.brittany-ferries.co.uk/guides/ports/portsmouth ♀ Wharf Road, Portsmouth PO2 8RU 📷 50.812 N, -1.087 W

KEY 🛳 Service operator *i* Info ♀ Location 📷 GPS ▬ Exit routes

Southern Europe

3

The Douro Valley, northern Portugal.

Cyprus

Cyprus gained its independence from the UK more than fifty years ago, but the island remains popular with British visitors. Reassuringly for them, Cyprus still drives on the left, and signposts, although sometimes erratic, are often in both Greek and English. There are good, four-lane motorways between Nicosia and the major cities of Limassol, Larnaca and Paphos; minor roads, however, are often unsurfaced. Take particular care around roadworks, as these may be poorly signed or unlit.

Foinikoudes Promenade in Larnaca. (Courtesy Philip Willcocks /Thinkstock)

In built-up areas, double yellow lines at the kerb indicate that parking and stopping are prohibited at all times; a single yellow line denotes that parking is prohibited, but loading and unloading are allowed. The police can levy on-the-spot fines, but cannot collect them. Drink-driving limits are severely enforced, with penalties including prison sentences and confiscation of the vehicle.

If you're hiring a car from one of the smaller, local companies, pay particular attention to its condition. Fortunately, the special number plates with a 'Z' prefix, which attracted thieves to hire cars, were dropped in 2013. Visitors may use their own cars for up to three months.

A police car joins in the fun at Limassol Carnival. (Courtesy jvoisey/Thinkstock)

Northern Cyprus

The northern part of Cyprus has been under Turkish control since 1974, but its authority is not internationally recognised. It has been possible to cross the 'Attila' or 'Green' Line between the two parts of the island since 2003, but visitors should

Crossing the border from the Turkish-controlled area of Cyprus in Nicosia. (Courtesy ciminieri/Thinkstock)

Cyprus

keep clear of the buffer zone around this line. Traffic rules are broadly the same as on the rest of the island, but insurance Green Cards are not recognised, so you'll need to take out insurance at the border crossing for your own car, or check that you can take a hire car across. In emergencies, call 112 for ambulance services only; use 155 to contact the police and 199 for fire services. See also parking signs in Greece (page 91).

Opening information for mountain road

Border with the Turkish occupied area of Northern Cyprus

SPEED LIMITS			km/h
🏘 Towns/villages	(50) / (30) in pedestrian zones		
🚗 Main roads	(65) / (80)		
🚦 Motorways	(100)		

Yellow box junction: do not enter unless your exit is clear

GENERAL RULES

⊤ Drink-drive limit (g/l blood)	0.5 / 0.2 for new drivers (first three years)	
Children in front seats	No children under five at all; 5-10 yo with suitable restraint	
Min driving age	18 (25, with licence held for min two years, to hire)	
Licence or IDP	✓	UK photocard or three-part pink licence recommended IDP required for green UK licence or non-EU licences
Insurance: Green Card	✓ Recommended	
DRL	○ Use in poor visibility	
Mobile phones	⊘ Handheld phones prohibited	
	✕ Hands-free tolerated, but not recommended	
📡 Radar detectors	⊘ Prohibited	
GPS speed camera alerts (POI)	⊘ Prohibited	
Emergency services	Call 112 or 199 (Republic of Cyprus)	
Special rules		

- Drive on the left
- Horn may not be used from 10pm to 6am or near hospitals
- Spotlights prohibited
- No eating or drinking whilst driving
- No smoking in cars with children under 16
- ALWAYS contact police in event of accident

Attention! Drive on the Left

Drive on the left!

Many road signs are in Greek and English

DRIVING EQUIPMENT

⚠ Warning triangle	○ Two required	
🦺 High-vis jacket(s)	✓ Recommended	
🩹 First-aid kit	✓ Recommended	
🧯 Fire extinguisher	✓ Recommended	
💡 Spare bulbs	✓ Recommended	
Spare fuel (can)	⊘ Prohibited	
⚙ Winter tyres	No special rules	
❄ Snow chains	⊘ Prohibited on motorways	
	✓ Permitted if required by conditions	

i www.drivetogether.eu/DefaultArticle/Article=1357

TOLLS

🚦 Free	
🅿 No other tolls	

Cyprus

Greece

The road to nowhere ... on the island of Lesbos. (Courtesy Stephen Eastop/Freeimages.com)

In the south-eastern corner of Europe, the roads through the Greek mainland are often crowded with a huge number of motorbikes and scooters, as well as trucks, heading to Asia. By the admission of its own traffic police, the quality of roads and driving standards often leave a lot to be desired, and road-building programmes are only now resuming after the recent economic austerity. Local drivers have some of the lowest rates in Europe for the use of seat belts and child restraints, but don't be tempted to follow their example!

Happily, driving on the islands or away from the main cities is much more relaxed, with many unspoilt and often empty roads to enjoy. Greek drivers flash their headlights to warn other drivers to get out of the way, and it's customary to pull over the white line at the side of the road to let cars overtake. On motorways, the hard shoulder is also sometimes used as a regular lane. Traffic entering a roundabout has priority, unless signs indicate otherwise.

Most of the restrictions you need to watch for apply only in the big cities. Access to Athens is controlled, but foreign-registered cars and hire cars are currently exempt. On-street parking, however, is very limited, and

The historic skyline of Athens. (Courtesy Greek National Tourism Organisation)

Look out for goats on the road! (Courtesy Ben van der Meer/Freeimages.com)

illegally parked cars may have their number plates confiscated by the police, effectively immobilising them! White lines on the road indicate that parking is allowed; blue lines that you must pay to park; and yellow lines that parking is prohibited. Parking is also forbidden within 12m (40ft) of a bus or tram stop, and within 20m (65ft) of traffic lights. The police can issue fines on-the-spot, but they should be paid – within ten days – at a Public Treasury office. Finally, wherever you go, note that LPG is available only for taxis.

Greece

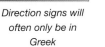

Direction signs will often only be in Greek

No parking during odd months of year (left), and even months of year

Speed limit (50km/h)

No parking

SPEED LIMITS			km/h
Towns/villages	50		
Main roads	70	90	
Motorways	110	130	reduced in the wet

GENERAL RULES		
Drink-drive limit (g/l blood)		0.5 / 0.2 for new drivers (first two years)
Children in front seats		Min 12 yo and 1.35m height, unless suitable restraint used
Min driving age		18 (21-25 to hire)
Licence or IDP	✓	UK photocard or three-part pink licence recommended; IDP required for green UK licence or non-EU licences, and by some car rental companies
Insurance: Green Card	✓	Recommended
DRL	O	Use in poor visibility
Mobile phones	⊘	Handheld phones prohibited
	✗	Hands-free tolerated, but not recommended
Radar detectors	⊘	Prohibited
GPS speed camera alerts (POI)	✗	Not recommended
Emergency services		Call 112
Special rules		

- Restricted access to Athens, Piraeus & Thessaloniki for diesel-engined vehicles
- Changing lanes at junctions prohibited
- No smoking in cars with children under 12
- Police must be called to accidents in case of injures or if vehicles block road

DRIVING EQUIPMENT		
Warning triangle	O	Required
High-vis jacket(s)	✓	Recommended
First-aid kit	O	Required
Fire extinguisher	O	Required
Spare bulbs	✓	Recommended
Spare fuel (can)	⊘	Prohibited
Winter tyres		No special rules
Snow chains	✓	Permitted if required by conditions

TOLLS		
Tolls on motorways		
How to pay		Pay on entry: cash/credit cards (some routes); electronic system not yet consolidated
		Aktion, Artemission & Charilaos Trikoupis bridges and tunnels

Italy

With its sunny climate, great food and wine, rich history, and beautiful scenery, what's not to like about Italy? For foreign motorists, it could be the experience of driving there, as that same relaxed attitude to life which ensures such a great holiday, can make for an unnerving experience behind the wheel. As one Italian politician, Antonio Martini, allegedly put it: "In Milan, traffic lights are instructions. In Rome, they are suggestions. In Naples, they are Christmas decorations." And in the land of Ferrari and Lamborghini, the Italians' love of speed is well known.

So, take a deep breath and stay calm. In cities, watch out for scooters everywhere, and – in summer especially, with windows open or a convertible hood down – keep handbags

Brown signs provide information on this area of natural beauty in Sicily. (Courtesy Fototeca ENIT)

and valuables hidden from view in traffic. When turning left at junctions, turn in front of the car turning left in the opposite lane. In many cities (including Florence, Genoa, Naples and Rome) access to the historic centres is strictly controlled: entry to so-called ZTLs ('Zone a Traffico Limitato') is restricted to residents, or – in the case of Bologna and Milan's Area C – permitted only by buying a special ticket. In Naples, there are access restrictions for cars without catalytic converters.

Away from the cities, the beautiful passes of the Dolomites (see page 94) and the gravelled 'white roads' of Tuscany, can prove demanding for your car. Further south, the stunning Amalfi coastal road is closed to camper vans and caravans. LPG can also be hard to find in the south.

Tourists threading their way through a narrow historic town. (Courtesy Avis)

The impressive span of the Pitigliano viaduct in western Tuscany.

San Marino and Vatican City

The rules for driving in San Marino are the same as in Italy, except that smoking is not allowed when driving. If you're visiting the Vatican, take a bus or walk: it only takes 20 minutes to cross on foot!

zona traffico limitato

Limited access to city centre

SPEED LIMITS

		km/h
🏠 Towns/villages	**50**	
🛣 Main roads	**90**	
🛣 Motorways	**130** / **150**	some three-lane m'ways
	110 in bad weather / **100** for new drivers	

GENERAL RULES

🍸	Drink-drive limit (g/l blood)	0.5 / 0.0 for new drivers (first three years)
👤	Children in front seats	For foreign-registered vehicles, legislation in home country applies. For local hire cars, min 1.5m height and 36kg, unless suitable restraint used
👥	Min driving age	18 (21 to hire)
✳	Licence or IDP	UK photocard or three-part pink licence recommended; IDP required for green UK licence or non-EU licences
🔲	Insurance: Green Card	✅ Recommended
☼	DRL	⭕ Required outside of built-up areas
📱	Mobile phones	⊘ Handhelds prohibited / ✖ Hands-free tolerated, but not recommended
📶	Radar detectors	⊘ Prohibited
📷	GPS speed camera alerts (POI)	✅ Allowed
➕	Emergency services	Police 112 or 113 / Fire 115 / Ambulance 118
🔧	Special rules	• Park facing direction of traffic • If carrying more than one pet, they must be secured

i www.aci.it/laci/driving-in-italy.html

Residential zone

Carabinieri (police)

Tunnel entrance

Multiple level crossings ('St Andrew's crosses')

School bus stop

DRIVING EQUIPMENT

⚠	Warning triangle	⭕	Required
🦺	High-vis jacket(s)	⭕	Required for driver & all passengers (keep inside car)
🧰	First-aid kit	✅	Recommended
🧯	Fire extinguisher	✅	Recommended
💡	Spare bulbs	✅	Recommended
⛽	Spare fuel (can)	✅	Allowed
❄	Winter tyres	⭕	Obligatory in Val d'Aosta, otherwise follow local regulations from 15/10 or 1/11 to 15/04
❄	Snow chains		Follow local regulations

TOLLS

🛣	Tolls on motorways	
💳	How to pay	Separate lanes for cash/credit cards/pre-paid card (Viacard)/tag (Telepass)

i

www.autostrade.it/en   www.tolltickets.com

🔆 Tunnels, including Great St Bernard, Mont Blanc, Munt la Schera

Italy

Mountain roads and tunnels

A breathtaking view of the Stelvio Pass. (Courtesy Nicola Bormolini/ENIT)

KEY ♀ → Location Statistics: height m / ft / max gradient 📅 When open ⚙ Toll 🚐 Caravans+trailers *i* Info

Aprica (SS39)
♀ Edolo → Tresenda 1176 / 3858 / 9% 📅 Normally open all year 🚐 Not recommended

Campolongo (SS244)
♀ Corvara in Badia → Arabba 1875 / 6152 / 10% 📅 Some closures Dec to Mar 🚐 Not recommended

Costalunga (SS241)
♀ Cardano → Pozza 1752 / 5748 / 12% 📅 Normally open all year 🚐 Prohibited

Erbe/Würzjoch (SP49)
♀ Brixen → St Martin in Thurn 1987 / 6519 / 16% 📅 Open mid-May to Nov 🚐 Prohibited

Falzarego (SR48)
♀ Cernadoi → Cortina d'Ampezzo 2117 / 6946 / 11% 📅 Some closures Dec to Apr 🚐 Not recommended

Fedaia (SS641)
♀ Canazei → Caprile 2057 / 6749 / 15% 📅 Some closures in winter 🚐 Not recommended

Foscagno (SS301)
♀ Livigno → Bormio 2291 / 7516 / 12% 📅 Some closures Nov to May 🚐 Not recommended

Gardena (SS243)
♀ Selva di Val Gardena → Corvara in Badia 2137 / 7011 / 16% 📅 Some closures Dec to Jun 🚐 Prohibited

Gavia (SS300)
♀ Ponte di Legbo → Bormio 2621 / 8599 / 16% 📅 Open Jun to Oct 🚐 Prohibited

Le Palade (SS238)

📍 Tesimo → Fondo 🏔 1518 / 4980 / 9% 📅 Normally open all year 🚐 Not recommended

 Mendola (SS42)

📍 Appiano → Cavareno 🏔 1363 / 4472 / 10% 📅 Normally open all year 🚐 Not recommended

 Monte Giovo/Jaufenpass (SS44)

📍 San Leonardo in Passina → Sterzing 🏔 2104 / 6903 / 12% 📅 Normally open all year; closed at night in winter 🚐 Prohibited

 Pennes/Penserjoch (SS518)

📍 Bozen (Bolzano) → Sterzing 🏔 2211 / 7254 / 13% 📅 Open Jun to mid-Nov 🚐 Prohibited

 Pordoi (SS48)

📍 Arabba → Canazei 🏔 2239 / 7346 / 8% 📅 Some closures Dec to Apr 🚐 Not recommended

 Résia/Reschenpass (SS40/B180)

📍 Resia/Reschen am See → Nauders (Austria) 🏔 1504 / 4934 / 9% 📅 Normally open all year 🚐 May be used

 Rolle (SS50)

📍 Mezzano → Predazzo 🏔 1989 / 6526 / 11% 📅 Some closures Dec to Mar 🚐 Not recommended

 San Pellegrino (SS346)

📍 Moena → Falcade 🏔 1918 / 6293 / 18% 📅 Normally open all year 🚐 Prohibited

 Sella (SS242)

📍 Canazei → Selva di Val Gardena 🏔 2240 / 7349 / 11% 📅 Some closures Dec to Jun 🚐 Prohibited

 Stelvio (SS38)

📍 Spondigna → Bormio 🏔 2757 / 9045 / 15% 📅 Open Jun to Oct 🚐 Prohibited

 Tonale (SS42)

📍 Ponte di Legno → Vermiglio 🏔 1883 / 6178 / 10% 📅 Normally open all year 🚐 May be used

Tre Croci (SR48)

📍 Cortina d'Ampezzo → Misurina 🏔 1809 / 5935 / 12% 📅 Some closures Dec to Mar 🚐 Not recommended

Italy

Current traffic information is available from:

www.oeamtc.at/portal/berg-passstrassen+2500++500408

Portugal

For many years, Portugal had a poor road safety record. In particular, there were many accidents in the southern Algarve region, popular with holidaymakers from abroad. For some foreign drivers, the unfamiliar 'priority to the right' rule, as found in other European countries such as France, probably contributed to these sad statistics.

Terraced hillsides in the Douro Valley, in northern Portugal.

Happily, the number of road deaths fell by half during the first decade of the 21st century, helped by the rapid development of the country's motorway network. Known as 'Autoestradas,' these now cover more than 2600km (1600 miles), and have reduced traffic congestion on many of Portugal's roads, although the first weekend in August is notorious for the high volume of traffic, as locals head off on holiday. Many of the Autoestradas are subject to tolls, with new electronic payment facilities being introduced (see Checklist). As in France, the temporary motorway toll devices from Via Verde can also be used in some car parks in major cities.

Rush hour traffic in Lisbon and Oporto can be especially heavy, and it's an offence to run out of fuel on the busy bridge over the Tagus. Parking can be hard to find in these cities. Blue zone parking areas are used in Lisbon, but parking meters are common elsewhere.

Old tram in Oporto.

There are heavy fines for illegal parking, and the police can issue tickets on-the-spot, and collect payment immediately with portable credit card devices.

In a bid to help Portuguese consumers save money, lower cost, additive-free fuels have recently been introduced at some filling stations, but you may want to check with the manufacturer of your car to see if this will cause any problem for your engine. Credit cards are widely accepted at major filling stations, but a surcharge may be applied for using one.

Portuguese motorway, showing the different lanes for electronic pass & cardholders. (Courtesy Via Verde)

Accident ahead

Reduced visibility

Use dipped headlights

End of prohibited parking

Electronic toll in 300m (on motorway)

Single level crossing ('St Andrew's cross')

SPEED LIMITS
km/h

🏠 Towns/villages	**50** / **20**	in some areas
🛣 Main roads	**90** / **100**	
🚏 Motorways	**120** / **90**	new drivers (first year)

GENERAL RULES

🍷 Drink-drive limit (g/l blood)	0.5 / 0.2 for new drivers (first three years)	
🧍 Children in front seats	Min 12 yo and 1.5m height, unless suitable restraint used	
👶 Min driving age	18	
✹ Licence or IDP	✅	UK photocard or three-part pink licence recommended; IDP required for green UK licence or non-EU licences
🪪 Insurance: Green Card	✅ Recommended	
⚙ DRL	⭕	Use in poor visibility; required on some motorways (as signed)
📱 Mobile phones	⊘	Handheld phones prohibited
	❌	Hands-free tolerated, but not recommended
📶 Radar detectors	⊘ Prohibited	
📡 GPS speed camera alerts (POI)	✅ Allowed	
➕ Emergency services	Call 112	
🔧 Special rules		

- Restricted access to historic centres of Lisbon & Gaia (Oporto)
- Dashcams prohibited
- Illegal to carry bikes on rear of car

DRIVING EQUIPMENT

⚠ Warning triangle	⭕	Required (inside car) for residents; recommended for visitors
🦺 High-vis jacket(s)	✅	Required (inside car) for residents; recommended for visitors
🧰 First-aid kit	✅	Recommended
🧯 Fire extinguisher	✅	Recommended
💡 Spare bulbs	✅	Recommended
⛽ Spare fuel (can)	⊘	Prohibited
⚙ Winter tyres	⊘	Studded tyres prohibited
❄ Snow chains		Permitted if required by conditions
🧳 Additional items	✅	Driver & all passengers must carry photo ID New drivers (first year) must display '90' sticker at rear of car

TOLLS

🚏 Tolls on motorways	
💳 How to pay	Most motorways: cash/credit cards; others: electronic payment only. Linked credit card & vehicle registration (Easytoll), pre-paid card (Tollcard) or temporary tag (Via Verde)
i	www.viaverde.pt

🔲 Lisbon: Vasco da Gama & 25 de Abril Bridges

Spain

Spain

Ever since the advent of package holidays in the 1970s, Spain has been a hugely popular holiday destination. If you're planning to drive from the UK, direct ferry crossings to Bilbao and Santander (see page 100) make for a much shorter drive. For foreign drivers worried about the hazards of driving there, Spain's road safety record has improved massively of late, with deaths in traffic accidents down by 66% from 2001 to 2012.

The road to Cap de Formentor on Majorca. (Courtesy MadrugadaVerde/Thinkstock)

Spain has many scenic routes to enjoy, such as those in the Picos de Europa or the roads around Ronda in the south. But watch your speed and be sure to indicate when changing lanes on motorways ('Autopistas'): for safety's sake, of course, but also to avoid the swingeing on-the-spot fines, which may exceed €300. When turning left at junctions, the Spanish do things 'Indonesian-style:' you must turn in front of the car turning left in the opposite lane.

Fifth Centenary Bridge in Seville. (Courtesy Carlos Koblischek/Freeimages.com)

There is limited availability of LPG (known as 'Autogas'): check www.aoglp.com for more details. 98 octane petrol is generally available only in major cities and on main routes. If your car uses diesel, be sure to fill up with Gasoleo A and not Gasoleo B, which is heating oil!

In many cities, parking is controlled in so-called blue zones ('zonas azul'), with the spaces where parking is allowed clearly marked on the road surface. Follow the signs to pay at a nearby

Traffic police on duty in Madrid. (Courtesy Richard McMillan/Freeimages.com)

machine and/or display a parking disc. In Madrid, some of these zones include separate low emission sections, where the price of the parking ticket depends on the age of the vehicle (and the emissions it is presumed to produce). Madrid is also expanding its 'Areas de Prioridad Residencial' (APR): access to these central areas is limited to residents, and visitors may only use the main thoroughfares in them.

Watch out for falling rocks!
(Courtesy Daniel Ernst/Thinkstock)

*Recommended
speed limit*

Tunnel entrance

*Headlights no longer
required (in daytime)*

*Pay machine in 'zona
azul' (blue zone)*

*No parking on Mon/
Weds/Fri/Sun*

*No parking on Tue/
Thu/Sat*

Spain

SPEED LIMITS
km/h

🏠	Towns/villages	(50)
🛣	Main roads	(90)
🛣	Motorways	(120)

GENERAL RULES

🍸	Drink-drive limit (g/l blood)	0.5; 0.3 for new drivers (first two years)
👶	Children in front seats	Min 12 yo and 1.35m height, unless suitable restraint used
⚖	Min driving age	18 (21 to hire)
✳	Licence or IDP	UK photocard or three-part pink licence recommended; IDP required for green UK licence
📇	Insurance: Green Card	Recommended
⚙	DRL	Required in poor visibility or contraflow systems only
📱	Mobile phones	Handheld phones and earphones prohibited / Hands-free must have Bluetooth connection
📶	Radar detectors	Prohibited
📷	GPS speed camera alerts (POI)	Allowed
➕	Emergency services	Call 112
🔧	Special rules	

- Flip-flops may not be worn when driving
- GPS units should not be programmed when driving

DRIVING EQUIPMENT

⚠	Warning triangle	○ Required (two for residents)
🦺	High-vis jacket(s)	○ Required
🧰	First-aid kit	✔ Recommended
🧯	Fire extinguisher	✔ Recommended
💡	Spare bulbs	✔ Recommended (required until recently)
⛽	Spare fuel (can)	✔ Allowed
❄	Winter tyres / Snow chains	✔ Use in heavy snow
🧳	Additional items	✔ Spare glasses or contact lenses if worn; spare wheel or puncture repair kit

TOLLS

🛣	Tolls on motorways	
💳	How to pay	Separate lanes for cash/credit cards/tag (Via T Bip & Drive)

www.autopistas.com/en   www.bipdrive.com/en/   www.tolltickets.com

i

🚇	Cadi Tunnel (French border) Vallvidrera Tunnel, Barcelona

Travelling to and from Spain

f you're heading to Spain or Portugal from the UK, the ferry services to northern Spain will save you a long drive through France. You can cross to Santander, the capital of Cantabria, or Bilbao, famed for its great seafood and the exceptional Guggenheim Museum.

Port information

Ferry operator contacts
Brittany Ferries   www.brittany-ferries.co.uk   +34 9 02 108 147

🚢 Bilbao

🚢 Brittany Ferries: UK – Portsmouth
i www.brittany-ferries.co.uk/guides/ports/bilbao   ♀ Terminal de Brittany Ferries, Puerto de Bilbao, Muelle 3, 48508 Bilbao   🖳 43.354 N, -3.070 W

KEY 🚢 Service operator *i* Info ♀ Location   🖳 GPS ▬ Exit routes

The spectacular Guggenheim Museum in Bilbao.

🚢 Santander

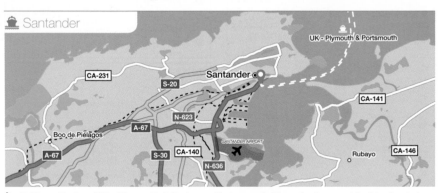

🚢 Brittany Ferries: UK – Plymouth & Portsmouth *i* www.brittany-ferries.co.uk/guides/ports/santander ♀ Estación Marítima, 39002 Santander   🖳 43.459 N, -3.806 W

Andorra

I t may be small – with an area of just 468 square kilometres (180 square miles) – but the tiny principality of Andorra is a hugely popular tourist destination. Each year it attracts over ten million visitors, who come for its great skiing in winter, and for hiking and mountain biking in summer. The nearest airports are at Barcelona and Perpignan, so you may well find yourself driving into the country. Andorra is famous, too, for its year-round duty-free shopping,

The Port d'Envalira Pass, which reaches 2408m (7900ft). (Courtesy Andorra Turisme)

so allow extra time for the frequent checks at the border crossings. If your car uses LPG, fill up in advance, as it's unavailable in Andorra.

At over 1000m (3300ft), Andorra-la-Vella is the highest capital in Europe, and mountains dominate the driving experience, with beautiful roads like the Pas de la Casa or the Coll d'Ordino. In many places, lower speed limits (40km/h in built-up areas, 60 or 70km/h outside) will be signposted, and the police can levy on-the-spot fines.

You'll need winter tyres in the ski season, and sometimes chains as well: look out for signs locally giving more information. In summer, watch out for cyclists weaving unsteadily in front of you as they head up the passes.

SPEED LIMITS		km/h
🏠 Towns/villages	**50**	See text
🛣 Main roads	**90**	

GENERAL RULES		
Ⴘ Drink-drive limit (g/l blood)	0.5	
♀ Children in front seats	Min 10 yo and 1.5m height, unless suitable restraint used	
👥 Min driving age	18 (19-21 to hire)	
✳ Licence or IDP	✓	UK photocard licence or IDP required
🖹 Insurance: Green Card	✓	Recommended
○ DRL	✓	Use in poor visibility
📱 Mobile phones	⊘	Handheld phones prohibited
	✕	Hands-free tolerated, but not recommended
📶 Radar detectors		Regulations unclear, but detectors prohibited in France & Spain, POI alerts also prohibited in France
📷 GPS speed camera alerts (POI)	✕	
✚ Emergency services	Call 110 (Police) 112 (Fire & Ambulance)	

DRIVING EQUIPMENT		
🔺 Warning triangle	○	Required (inside car)
🦺 High-vis jacket(s)	○	Required (inside car)
🧰 First-aid kit	✓	Recommended
🧯 Fire extinguisher	✓	Recommended
💡 Spare bulbs	○	Required
🛢 Spare fuel (can)	⊘	Prohibited
⚙ Winter tyres	✓	Recommended
❄ Snow chains	✓	Required according to conditions/as signed
🧳 Additional items	○	GB sticker for UK-registered cars (even with EU-type number plates)

TOLLS	
🚏 No motorway tolls	
🔲 Envalira Tunnel (from France)	
i	www.tuneldenvalira.com/index.php/en/

Gibraltar

Only a humorist like Peter Ustinov could have imagined squeezing a Grand Prix race onto Gibraltar's crowded streets. A mere seven square kilometres (2.7 square miles) in area, this little corner of Britain – where English is spoken and sterling accepted – reputedly has one of the world's highest levels of car ownership. If you

Looking down on Gibraltar.
(Courtesy The Gibraltar Tourist Board)

are just visiting the territory itself, flying there and using the local buses and cable car up to the Rock is probably the best option. If you are touring southern Spain, though, you may well want to stop at this popular tourist destination.

Gibraltar's Highway Code is largely based on that of the UK, but with the one big difference that you drive on the right, and with a good dash of Mediterranean brio added! There can be delays at the border crossing at La Linea, especially when so-called 'enhanced checks' are in place. You can check the current situation on Twitter (@gibraltarborder) or via the webcams at www.frontierqueue.gi. Once you're in, it's best to park outside the city walls, in one of the multi-storey car parks (on Grand Parade or Queensway, or in the International Commercial Centre). Note too that LPG is unavailable.

SPEED LIMITS	km/h
Towns/villages	50

GENERAL RULES	
Drink-drive limit (g/l blood)	0.8
Children in front seats	Min 12 yo and 1.35m height, unless suitable restraint used
Min driving age	18
Licence or IDP	✓ All UK licences accepted, but photocard or three-part pink license recommended
Insurance: Green Card	○ Required
DRL	○ Use in poor visibility
Mobile phones	⊘ Handheld phones prohibited
	✗ Hands-free tolerated, but not recommended
Radar detectors	
GPS speed camera alerts (POI)	No current legislation
Emergency services	Call 112
Special rules	
• Use of main beam headlights prohibited	
i www.visitgibraltar.gi/faqs	

DRIVING EQUIPMENT		
Warning triangle	○	Required
High-vis jacket(s)	✓	Recommended
First-aid kit	✓	Recommended
Fire extinguisher	✓	Recommended
Spare bulbs	✓	Recommended
Spare fuel (can)	✓	Allowed (duty payable)
Winter tyres		No special regulations
Snow chains		

TOLLS		
No motorways		Upper Rock Road

Malta

Malta gained independence from the United Kingdom in 1964, but British influences are still strong. English is spoken by nearly everyone, and the island is popular with British visitors. You can also take a car ferry to the neighbouring island of Gozo.

If you plan to rent a car, Malta drives on the left, and the Highway Code is based on that in the UK. Local drivers take a more relaxed approach to driving, however, often failing to indicate when changing direction, for example. Most of Malta's roads are asphalted, but surfaces can be poor in more remote areas. On narrow roads, the

Country road on Malta. (Courtesy www.viewingmalta.com/ Nina Adams)

driver of the car nearer to the wider section of road should give way. Access to Valletta is restricted (see Checklist), and traffic can also be heavy in Victoria, the main town on Gozo. If you're planning a weekend trip, be aware that most petrol stations are closed on Sundays.

If you have the misfortune to have an accident, there's a special form for front-to-rear collisions, similar to the European Accident Statement Form, which all local drivers and car rental companies should have. You should inform the police and wait until they arrive before moving the vehicles involved.

SPEED LIMITS	km/h
🏠 Towns/villages	**50**
🛣 Main roads	**80**

GENERAL RULES	
⏷ Drink-drive limit (g/l blood)	0.8
👤 Children in front seats	Min 10 yo and 1.5m height, unless suitable restraint used
👪 Min driving age	18 (often 21 to hire)
✳ Licence or IDP	✓ UK photocard or three-part pink licence recommended
▤ Insurance: Green Card	✓ Recommended
⚙ DRL	○ Required
📱 Mobile phones	⊘ Handheld phones prohibited
	✕ Hands-free tolerated, but not recommended
📶 Radar detectors GPS speed camera alerts (POI)	No current regulations
➕ Emergency services	Call 112
📞 Accidents	Report non-injury road accidents on + 356 21 32 02 02
⚒ Special rules	
	• Drive on the left
	• Priority lane reserved for public transport and emergency service vehicles
	• Spot lights prohibited
i	www.transport.gov.mt/roads-infrastructure/the-highway-code

DRIVING EQUIPMENT	
⚠ Warning triangle	○ Required
🦺 High-vis jacket(s)	✓ Recommended
🧰 First-aid kit	○ Required
🔥 Fire extinguisher	○ Required
💡 Spare bulbs	✓ Recommended
⛽ Spare fuel (can)	⚠ Prohibited on ferries, otherwise allowed
❄ Winter tyres	No special regulations
❄ Snow chains	
🧳 Additional items	○ GB sticker for all UK-registered cars (even with EU-type number plates)

TOLLS	
🚷 No motorways	
🅿 Permit required to enter Valletta; park & ride service available	

Turkey

A sunny coastal road. (Courtesy Sergey Mostovoy/Thinkstock)

It will be an adventurous driver indeed who drives all the way from northern Europe to Istanbul, at the gateway to Asia. But Turkey is a popular holiday destination, so you may well want to hire a car to explore its historic sites or beautiful coastal scenery. Most of the country is trouble-free, but the British Foreign Office advises against travelling within 10km (6 miles) of the border with Syria, and to some remote areas (see www.gov.uk/foreign-travel-advice/turkey).

However you come, driving in Turkey is not for the faint-hearted. Conditions can be dangerous, especially in Istanbul and Ankara, with local drivers often speeding or making risky overtaking manoeuvres. Standards are improving, but many motorcyclists received inadequate

Heavy traffic in Istanbul. (Courtesy ESezer/Thinkstock)

training in the past. Resist the temptation to join the melee, and drive defensively, so that you can stay out of trouble. At roundabouts, traffic entering from the right has priority, unless there are 'Stop' or 'Give Way' signs on the approach.

Traffic in Istanbul can be very heavy, although plans are underway to build a new 6.5km (4 miles) triple-deck tunnel under the Bosporus, which should open in 2020 and ease some of the congestion. The country's motorway network is also set to be privatised and expand, improving connections between the major cities.

Away from towns, road surfaces can be very poor, with potholes sometimes causing drivers to swerve unexpectedly. Rain and mud can make already poor surfaces especially slippery. Livestock on the road can also be a hazard, especially at night.

Crashed car in the river bed.
(Courtesy lilly3/Thinkstock)

If you are involved in an accident, cars with bodywork damage may be checked by the police to ensure they are safe to drive before being allowed to leave the country. The police can also levy on-the-spot fines.

Turkey

SPEED LIMITS	km/h
🏠 Towns/villages	**50**
🛣 Main roads	**90**
🛣 Motorways	**120**

GENERAL RULES

🍷 Drink-drive limit (g/l blood)	0.5; 0.0 for drivers of caravans or trailers	
👶 Children in front seats	Min 12 yo, 1.5m height and 36kg, unless suitable restraint used	
⚓ Min driving age	18 (21-25 to hire car, with licence held for min two years)	
✳ Licence or IDP	✓	IDP required for non-photocard licences and for stays over 90 days; recommended for all drivers
📋 Insurance: Green Card	○	Required: must cover European & Asian parts of country, or take out local insurance at border
✪ DRL	○	Use in poor visibility
📱 Mobile phones	⊘	Handheld phones prohibited
	✕	Hands-free tolerated, but not recommended
📶 Radar detectors	⊘	Prohibited
📷 GPS speed camera alerts (POI)	✕	Not recommended
➕ Emergency services	Police 155 Fire 110 Ambulance 112	
⚒ Special rules		

- All accidents must be reported to police and report obtained
- Use of horn prohibited from 10pm until sunrise

DUR
Stop!

TEK YÖN
One-way street

P
Park with wheels on pavement

GÜMRÜK DOUANE
Stop at customs post

DRIVING EQUIPMENT

🔺 Warning triangle	A	○	Two required
🦺 High-vis jacket(s)		✓	Recommended
🧰 First-aid kit		○	Required
🧯 Fire extinguisher		○	Required for residents; recommended for visitors
💡 Spare bulbs		✓	Recommended
⛽ Spare fuel (can)		✓	Allowed (max 25L)
⚙ Winter tyres		⊘	Studded tyres prohibited
❄ Snow chains		✓	Use according to conditions
🧳 Additional items		○	Spare wheel or puncture repair kit

TOLLS

🛣 Tolls on motorways	
💳 How to pay	Electronic payment system (HGS): buy sticker ('Vignette') or pre-paid card from post offices & filling stations
💳	Fatih Sultan Mehmet & Bogazici Bridges over Bosporus

Northern Europe

4

On the road in Iceland.
(Courtesy Visit Iceland)

Iceland

For the adventurous traveller, Iceland has some of Europe's most beautiful roads ... and also some of the safest, with accident rates among the lowest in the world. Drink-driving rules are strictly enforced and the police can levy high, on-the-spot fines for other offences.

Whilst the major roads are paved, watch out when the surface changes to gravel, as it's easy to lose traction. To get around much of the island, a four-wheel drive (4WD) vehicle with good ground clearance is essential; note, however, that LPG is not available. River crossings are common, so check first if you're unsure of the depth. Look out, too, for sheep on the road, narrow bridges, and blind crests, and be sure to keep to the marked tracks. Weather conditions change quickly, and in winter there can be delays in clearing snow. Some roads in the highlands open as late as July.

SPEED LIMITS
km/h

🏠 Towns/villages	**50** / **30**	in residential zones
🛣 Main roads	**80**	on gravel roads
	90	on asphalt

GENERAL RULES

🍸	Drink-drive limit (g/l blood)	0.5
🧍	Children in front seats	Min 3 yo and 1.5m height, unless suitable restraint used. Airbag must be deactivated
👥	Min driving age	17
✳	Licence or IDP	✔ UK photocard or three-part pink licence recommended IDP required for UK green licences and non-EU licences Temporary licence may be obtained locally on presentation of UK licence
▭	Insurance: Green Card	✔ Recommended
⚙	DRL	○ Dipped headlights required
📱	Mobile phones	⊘ Handheld phones prohibited ⊗ Hands-free tolerated, but not recommended
📶	Radar detectors	⊘ Prohibited
📷	GPS speed camera alerts (POI)	✔ Allowed
➕	Emergency services	112
🔧	Special rules	

- Police must be called to all accidents involving injury
- Traffic on roundabout has priority
- No parking allowed within 5m (16ft) of junctions and 15m (50ft) of bus stops

i www.icetra.is/road-traffic/how-to-drive-in-iceland/ Phone 1777 for information on road conditions

MALBIK ENDAR

End of paved road

Deaf people present

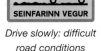

SEINFARINN VEGUR

Drive slowly: difficult road conditions

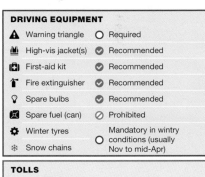

ÓBRÚAÐAR ÁR

Ford: only suitable for 4WD

DRIVING EQUIPMENT

🔺	Warning triangle	○	Required
🦺	High-vis jacket(s)	✔	Recommended
🧰	First-aid kit	✔	Recommended
🧯	Fire extinguisher	✔	Recommended
💡	Spare bulbs	✔	Recommended
⛽	Spare fuel (can)	⊘	Prohibited
⚙	Winter tyres	○	Mandatory in wintry conditions (usually Nov to mid-Apr)
❄	Snow chains		

TOLLS

💳	Hvalfjördur Tunnel
i	www.spolur.is

Denmark

There is no longer a direct ferry service from Harwich to Esbjerg, so it's now a longer drive for UK visitors to Denmark, up through Holland and northern Germany. But travelling in Denmark is an easy introduction to driving in Scandinavia: the terrain is gentler than in the other Nordic countries and, in winter, weather conditions are less severe. If you have come from Germany, speeds will seem much lower and – as throughout Scandinavia – drivers are generally courteous and disciplined, with low overall accident rates. The police can issue on-the-spot fines and have powers to hold cars until they are settled.

Half-timbered houses on Funen are reminiscent of England. (Courtesy Visit Denmark/John Sommer)

Many of Denmark's finest attractions lie along the scenic Marguerite-route, identified by signs with a daisy on a brown background (see page 109). To cover longer distances, Denmark's motorways are free, but there are tolls on a couple of major bridges, like the one between Copenhagen and Malmö, in Sweden. If you're also travelling in Norway, the Norwegian Autopass tag can be used on this bridge. Other connections between Denmark's main islands are assured by ferries, which can be crowded, so you may need to book in advance in summer.

In Copenhagen and Denmark's other major cities, look out for the numerous cyclists,

An unspoilt road in the Funen countryside. (Courtesy Visit Denmark/Bob Krist)

The Lillte Belt Bridge. (Courtesy Visit Denmark/ Cees van Roeden

Denmark

and be prepared to give way to traffic approaching from the right, unless there are Give Way or Stop signs. Most Danish cities are relatively small, so consider parking your car for the day (parking discs are widely used), and getting around with public transport, on foot, or renting a bicycle. Low pollution zones have been introduced in several Danish cities, but at present the restrictions only apply to diesel-engined vehicles over 3.5 tonnes. Drivers of LPG-powered cars should note that there is only limited availability of LPG.

4WD on the beach. (Courtesy Visit Denmark/ Mikkel Grabowski)

SPEED LIMITS
km/h

Towns/villages	**50** / **40**	central Copenhagen
Main roads	**80**	
Motorways	**110** / **130**	(reduced in the wet)

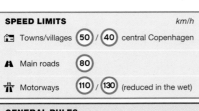

GENERAL RULES

Drink-drive limit (g/l blood)	0.5	
Children in front seats	Min 3 yo and 1.35m height, unless suitable restraint used	
Min driving age	18 (23-25 to hire, with licence for at least six months)	
Licence or IDP	●	UK photocard or three-part pink licence recommended If licence not in Roman type, IDP required
Insurance: Green Card	●	Recommended
DRL	○	Required
Mobile phones	⊘	Handheld phones prohibited
	✕	Hands-free tolerated, but not recommended
Radar detectors	⊘	Prohibited
GPS speed camera alerts (POI)	●	Allowed
Emergency services	112	
Special rules		

- All accidents involving injury or disputed responsibility must be reported to police
- Merge in turn when joining motorway
- Give way to buses and cycles
- Always park on right (in direction of traffic)
- No parking within 10m (33ft) of junction
- Camping Card International (CCI) required to use campsites

i www.visitdenmark.com/denmark/ driving-gdk478603

Ensrettet
One-way street

Place of interest

No through way for cars; cycle path continues

Merging traffic

Pass either side

Marguerite (touring) route

DRIVING EQUIPMENT

⚠	Warning triangle	○	Required
📛	High-vis jacket(s)	●	Recommended
🧰	First-aid kit	●	Recommended
🧯	Fire extinguisher	●	Recommended
💡	Spare bulbs	●	Recommended
⛽	Spare fuel (can)	⚠	Prohibited on ferries, otherwise allowed
⚙	Winter tyres	○	Winter tyres required according to conditions 1 Nov-15 Apr
❄	Snow chains		
🧳	Additional items	⚠	RHD cars and vehicles towing trailer must have exterior mirrors on both sides

TOLLS

🛣	Free	
	🏧	Øresund & Storebaelt bridges
🚪	How to pay	Cash or tag

i www.tolltickets.com

Denmark

Finland

Finland

The scenic roads of Finland make for some fantastic drives, but a little extra planning will help you make the most of your trip. Some forest roads shown on GPS devices may only be suitable for 4WD vehicles, so check a paper map, or with the locals, first. In the north, distances between filling stations can be as great as 100km (62 miles), and fuel may be more expensive. E10 petrol is sold throughout Finland, but LPG is not available.

Driving lights on all year throughout the Nordic region. (Courtesy Visit Finland)

Traffic jams are rare in Finland, but you may find yourself inadvertently sharing the road with elk or reindeer! Take special care at dusk and in May and October, when they most often venture onto the roads. Finnish drivers often flash their headlights to warn of animals ahead. Any accidents involving animals must be reported to the police. Winter conditions can be harsh, often leaving minor roads with frost damage. Many Finnish motorists equip their cars with parking heaters, allowing them to warm the engine block and car interior before starting off.

Finland holds the record for the highest speeding fines in the world. Fines are linked directly to the offender's income, with one multi-millionaire having been fined in excess of €100,000! Foreign drivers have been charged a much lower, standard amount, but with increasing cross-border cooperation in the EU, it's likely that the Finnish authorities will be able to obtain details of their income too. Even standard parking fines – payable at banks – run to over €100. To stay legal, parking discs – available from kiosks and petrol stations – are widely used. In some towns, streets are cleaned on specific days, and all cars must be removed. Finally, in Finland too, traffic from the right has the right of way, unless signs state otherwise.

Beware icy roads during the long Finnish winter. (Courtesy Visit Finland)

A main road in the eerie half-light.
(Courtesy Visit Finland)

No entry for snowmobiles

Detour

Elks on road

Reindeer on road

Frost
damage

Sign applies Mon-Fri
0800-1700

SPEED LIMITS   km/h

🏠 Towns/villages	**50** / **30**	in residential zones
🛣 Main roads	**80**	
🛣 Motorways	**120** Apr-Sep / **100** Oct-Mar	

GENERAL RULES

🍸 Drink-drive limit (g/l blood)	0.5; Åland Islands: 0.2 (planned reduction)
🚸 Children in front seats	Min 3 yo and 1.35m height, unless suitable restraint used
👥 Min driving age	18 (19-25 to rent car, with licence held at least one year)
✳ Licence or IDP	✔ UK photocard or three-part pink licence recommended
📇 Insurance: Green Card	✔ Recommended
☼ DRL	○ Dipped headlights required
📱 Mobile phones	⊘ Handheld phones prohibited
	✖ Hands-free tolerated, but not recommended
📡 Radar detectors	⊘ Prohibited
📷 GPS speed camera alerts (POI)	✔ Allowed
➕ Emergency services	112
🔧 Special rules	

- Trams and buses always have priority
- In towns, only use horn in case of immediate danger
- Use parking lights at night on unlit streets
- Turn off engine if stationary for two minutes or more (four minutes at -15°C or less)

ℹ www.expat-finland.com/living_in_finland/driving.html

Sign applies Sat
0800-1300

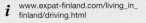

Sign applies Sun
0800-1400

DRIVING EQUIPMENT

⚠ Warning triangle	○	Required
🦺 High-vis jacket(s)	○	Required: all pedestrians must wear reflective clothing at night
🧰 First-aid kit	✔	Recommended
🧯 Fire extinguisher	○	Required for motor caravans, otherwise recommended
💡 Spare bulbs	✔	Recommended
⛽ Spare fuel (can)	⚠	Allowed (max 10L) if fire extinguisher carried
⚙ Winter tyres	○	Mandatory (min 3mm tread depth) 1 Dec-28 Feb (recommended Nov to Apr)
❄ Snow chains		
🧳 Additional items	○	Jack (recommended) Vehicles towing trailer must have exterior mirrors on both sides

TOLLS

🛣	Free
🅾	None

Norway

I f ever a country's roads were designed for unhurried exploration, it must be those of Norway ... Often narrow and twisting, they sometimes only have passing places for oncoming traffic. Some mountain roads are closed to caravans; in other places, fjord crossings by boat add to the fun of the journey. As a result, average speeds are low, so allow plenty of time for your journey.

Stopping for a break in Aure. (Courtesy CH/Visitnorway.com)

One of Norway's most famous roads is the Trollstigen Route or Trolls' Path: you might not meet any of these mythical creatures, but elk and deer are real hazards on Norwegian roads. There are lots of tunnels too, sometimes poorly lit, and in winter the weather makes road closures inevitable. If you are planning a winter trip to Norway with a diesel-engined car, fill up after you arrive, as Norwegian winter diesel is specially formulated to cope with temperatures as low as -32°C (-26°F). Some filling stations in more remote areas only accept cash, and there is limited availability of LPG.

Norway has an enviable road safety record, thanks in part to stringent fines (up to 10% of annual income for residents) and a very low drink-driving limit, which is rigorously enforced. Even if you leave your car safely parked-up for a night's socialising, be especially aware of the alcohol which may remain in your system the morning after.

Traffic on roundabouts has the right of way, but at other junctions, vehicles coming from the right normally have priority. Electric cars have been very successful in Norway, and can use the bus lanes in cities such as Oslo. Disabled drivers, meanwhile, are exempt from the tolls on some city ring roads.

At the time of going to press, plans are underway to revive a direct ferry crossing from the UK to Norway.

The many ferry crossings on Norway's fjords are an integral part of the country's transport network. (Courtesy Espen Mills/Tasteofnationaltouristroutes.com/Visitnorway.com) / Making the most of Norway's scenic routes with a detailed map. (Courtesy Terje Rakke/Nordic Life AS – Visitnorway.com)

Traffic joining merges in turn

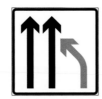

Traffic in ending lane must give way

Ski runs cross road

Moose

Viewpoint

Car pool lane

Passing place (Møteplass)

Norway

SPEED LIMITS   km/h

🏠 Towns/villages	**50** / **30**	in residential zones
🅰 Main roads	**80**	
🚏 Motorways	**90** / **100**	reduced in the wet

GENERAL RULES

🍸 Drink-drive limit (g/l blood)	0.2	
🧍 Children in front seats	Min 4 yo, height 1.5m, 36kg, unless suitable restraint used; booster cushion for children from 1.35-1.5m	
👪 Min driving age	18 (licence must be held for at least one year to hire)	
✳ Licence or IDP	✓	UK photocard or three-part pink licence recommended. IDP required for stays over three months
🖥 Insurance: Green Card	✓	Recommended
⭕ DRL	◯	Dipped headlights required
📱 Mobile phones	⊘	Handheld phones prohibited
	⊗	Hands-free tolerated, but not recommended
📶 Radar detectors	⊘	Prohibited
📟 GPS speed camera alerts (POI)	✓	Allowed
➕ Emergency services	Police 112 Fire 110 Ambulance 113	
🔧 Special rules		

- Trams always have priority
- Oslo: electric vehicles may use bus lanes
- Do not drink alcohol for six hours following any traffic incident which may be investigated by police

i www.visitnorway.com/uk/about-norway/safety-first/driving-in-norway/

DRIVING EQUIPMENT

🅰 Warning triangle	◯	Required
🦺 High-vis jacket(s)	◯	Required (inside car) for residents, recommended for visitors
🧰 First-aid kit	✓	Recommended
🧯 Fire extinguisher	✓	Recommended
💡 Spare bulbs	✓	Recommended
⛽ Spare fuel (can)	⚠	Prohibited on ferries, otherwise allowed (max 10L)
⚙ Winter tyres	◯	Winter tyres mandatory (3mm min tread depth) on all wheels when snow and ice on road
❄ Snow chains		
🧳 Additional items	◯	Torch recommended If towing, extension mirrors on both sides

TOLLS

🚏 Motorway tolls		
💳 How to pay	Nearly all tolls fully automated: register online for invoice, temporary tag or prepaid card	
i	www.autopass.no	
🅾 Tolls to enter major city centres		
💳 How to pay	In advance at petrol stations Hire cars must be registered online in advance (ask rental company)	

113

Sweden

I n most countries, being flashed by a traffic camera can only mean bad news. But in Sweden, the authorities tested a novel concept: cars travelling below the speed limit were photographed, and their drivers could win prizes financed by the proceeds of speeding fines! If you do commit a traffic

The Munkedal Bridge in Sweden, under construction. (Courtesy Per Pixel Petersson/imagebanksweden.se)

offence, the police can issue on-the-spot fines, which must be paid immediately or at a bank within a couple of weeks.

Sweden's roads are among the safest in the world, but in summer, the long daylight hours and vast distances can encourage drivers to travel further than is safe, with the risk of falling asleep at the wheel. Half of Sweden is covered in forests, so moose and deer are a frequent hazard; if you hit one of them, you must call the police. In winter, you may be surprised how fast the locals drive, but with mandatory winter tyres and plenty of practice, Swedish drivers are well prepared for icy conditions.

Lights on at all times. (Courtesy Fredrik Broman/imagebanksweden.se)

On roads with two or more lanes in each direction, and a speed limit of 70km/h (43mph) or less, overtaking on the right ('undertaking') is also allowed. Traffic on roundabouts has the right of way, but at other junctions vehicles coming from the right normally have priority. As in Finland, city streets are sometimes cleaned on specific days (shown on signs) and all cars must be removed. Parking on alternate sides of the street (see illustration opposite) is a common practice.

A legacy of Saab's last production models, bioethanol (E85) – designed for flex-fuel cars – is widely available, whereas LPG is rare, and diesel less popular than in many countries. In the north, there can be long distances between filling stations.

A peaceful country road in Sweden. (Courtesy Goran Assner/ imagebanksweden.se)

Accident

No vehicles with studded tyres

All way stop

Blind people crossing

Alternate-side parking ('Datumparkering')

No entry for any vehicles

Maximum recommended speed

End of maximum recommended speed

Sweden

SPEED LIMITS   km/h

Towns/villages	(50) / (20) or (30)	in some areas
Main roads	(70)	
Motorways	(90) / (110)	

GENERAL RULES

Drink-drive limit (g/l blood)	0.2
Children in front seats	Min 1.35m height, unless suitable restraint used; passenger airbag must be deactivated for children under 1.4m
Min driving age	18
Licence or IDP	✓ UK photocard or three-part pink licence recommended. Photo ID or IDP required for UK green licences
Insurance: Green Card	✓ Recommended
DRL	O Required; dipped headlights preferred
Mobile phones	⊘ Handheld phones prohibited
	✗ Hands-free tolerated, but not recommended
Radar detectors	⊘ Prohibited
GPS speed camera alerts (POI)	✓ Allowed
Emergency services	112
Special rules	

- Use of dashcams not recommended
- Trams always have priority
- No parking within 10m (33ft) of junction or pedestrian crossing
- Datumparkering: parking on odd-numbered side of road on odd days, and on even-numbered side on even days

i www.visitsweden.com/sweden/ Travel-guide/Getting-around-in-Sweden/By-Car/Driving-in-Sweden

DRIVING EQUIPMENT

Warning triangle	O	Required for residents, recommended for visitors
High-vis jacket(s)	✓	Recommended
First-aid kit	✓	Recommended
Fire extinguisher	✓	Recommended
Spare bulbs	✓	Recommended
Spare fuel (can)	⚠	Allowed (max 30L, but only 10L imported duty-free)
Winter tyres Snow chains	O	Winter tyres mandatory (min 3mm tread depth) 1 Dec to 31 Mar
Additional items	O	Antifreeze for screenwash Snow shovel (required) Tow rope and jump leads (recommended)

TOLLS

Free	
congestion charge	Stockholm & Göteborg: weekday daytime congestion charge Øresund, Svinesund, Motala & Sundsvall Bridges
How to pay	Automated number plate recognition & invoicing system

i www.epass24.com

Central & Eastern Europe

The remarkable Transfăgărășan Highway in Romania.
(Courtesy Romania Tourism)

Albania

For long cut off from visitors from Western Europe, Albania remains a largely unknown country. Its road network is gradually being overhauled, but away from the major routes conditions can be poor, with the risk of flash floods and power cuts taking out street lights. A four-wheel drive vehicle will often be the best way to reach some more remote places, and all drivers should allow extra travel time. Breakdown recovery services are limited, so taking a basic toolkit and spares is a sensible precaution.

Local drivers can seem aggressive, and in rural areas horse-drawn carts are still common, so take extra care, especially at night. Many road signs are similar to those in Italy (see page 93), which is one less challenge to overcome. If you do fall foul of the local rules, the police can levy on-the-spot fines up to 5000 ALL.

SPEED LIMITS		*km/h*
Towns/villages	40	
Main roads	80 / 90	
Motorways	110	

GENERAL RULES	
Drink-drive limit (g/l blood)	0.1
Children in front seats	Min 12 yo, unless suitable restraint used. Under 4s must travel in rear
Min driving age	18 (21 with licence held for at least one year to hire)
Licence or IDP	○ IDP required
Insurance: Green Card	○ Required
DRL	○ Required
Mobile phones	⊘ Handheld phones prohibited
	✕ Hands-free tolerated, but not recommended
Radar detectors	Not recommended (information not available)
GPS speed camera alerts (POI)	✕
Emergency services	Police 129 Ambulance 127 Fire 128
Special rules	• Priority to the right: give way to vehicles approaching from the right (unless signs indicate otherwise) • Use horn only in emergency or to overtake outside built-up areas • Call police to report all accidents

Danger: risk of flooding

Horizontal traffic lights

No entry to hand-drawn vehicles

zonë më
trafik të kufizuar

Restricted access zone

DRIVING EQUIPMENT		
Warning triangle	○	Required
High-vis jacket(s)	✓	Recommended
First-aid kit	○	Required
Fire extinguisher	○	Required
Spare bulbs	○	Required
Spare fuel (can)		Information not available
Winter tyres	✓	Recommended in wintry conditions
Snow chains		
Additional items	✓	Recommended: inventory of caravan/trailer contents Nationality sticker (even with Euro-style number plate)

TOLLS	
Free at present, but charges may be introduced later	
⊙ Exit tax payable on leaving country	

Armenia

Armenia

Formerly part of the Soviet Union, Armenia belongs geographically to Asia, but is a member of the Council of Europe and has close political and economic ties with Europe. Travelling by road into Armenia demands some extra planning: there are still diplomatic tensions in the region, and the border crossings with Turkey and Azerbaijan are subject to closures. Before you go, check with your insurer whether your cover can be extended to Armenia.

Although gradually improving, roads away from the main routes are often in poor condition, with ruts – especially after heavy rain – a particular danger. Watch out, too, for signs of falling rocks. The Armenian language uses its own alphabet of some 40 characters, but many road signs also give directions in a Roman script. Whichever script is used, however, signage can be inadequate, and a good local map is more than usually important.

If you're driving in cities such as the capital, Yerevan, broken traffic lights sometimes add to the hazards which motorists face, and – as in many countries in this chapter of the guide – local drivers can appear reckless to visitors used to the safer roads of Western Europe.

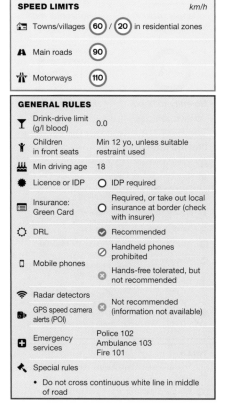

SPEED LIMITS		km/h
🏠 Towns/villages	**60** / **20** in residential zones	
🅰 Main roads	**90**	
🚏 Motorways	**110**	

GENERAL RULES	
⅄ Drink-drive limit (g/l blood)	0.0
🧍 Children in front seats	Min 12 yo, unless suitable restraint used
♛ Min driving age	18
✴ Licence or IDP	○ IDP required
▤ Insurance: Green Card	○ Required, or take out local insurance at border (check with insurer)
⚙ DRL	✔ Recommended
📱 Mobile phones	⊘ Handheld phones prohibited ✖ Hands-free tolerated, but not recommended
📶 Radar detectors GPS speed camera alerts (POI)	✖ Not recommended (information not available)
➕ Emergency services	Police 102 Ambulance 103 Fire 101
🔧 Special rules	• Do not cross continuous white line in middle of road

ԿԱՆԳ STOP

Stop

300 մ

Distance (300m)

30 րոպե

Parking restricted to 30 minutes

ԹՈՍԻ
🚫
7.00 – 19.00

No parking (during marked times)

DRIVING EQUIPMENT		
🅰 Warning triangle	○	Required (inside car)
👷 High-vis jacket(s)	✔	Recommended
🧰 First-aid kit	○	Required
🧯 Fire extinguisher	○	Required
💡 Spare bulbs	✔	Recommended
⛽ Spare fuel (can)	✔	Allowed: declare on entry
⚙ Winter tyres		
❄ Snow chains	○	Recommended Nov-Feb
🧳 Additional items	○	Nationality sticker (even with Euro-style number plate) Carnet de Passage en Douane recommended

TOLLS	
🚏 Free	

Azerbaijan

Straddling the border between Europe and Asia, two-thirds of Azerbaijan is rich in natural resources of oil and gas, and the country is a major location for petroleum exploration and production. Unsurprisingly, fuel is cheap by European standards, although there can be considerable distances between filling stations away from the capital, Baku: be sure to keep your tank filled up or carry some spare fuel in a can.

Only half of Azerbaijan's extensive road network is asphalted, and many stretches can become impassable after heavy rain or snow. If you're venturing away from the major cities, a four-wheel drive vehicle is essential, and you may want to hire a local driver or guide who's used to the terrain.

As in Armenia, policies issued by UK and other Western European insurers rarely extend to Azerbaijan, so you'll need to take out insurance for your stay at the border. The crossings with Armenia are liable to closures, so if you intend to drive into the country, seek advice from the embassy or consulate, and plan your route thoroughly, well in advance.

Accident ahead

Use dipped headlights

Diversion (road closed)

SPEED LIMITS		km/h
🏠 Towns/villages	**60**	
🛣 Main roads	**90**	

Oncoming traffic must give way

GENERAL RULES		
Drink-drive limit (g/l blood)	0.0	
Children in front seats	Min 12 yo, unless suitable restraint used	
Min driving age	18	
Licence or IDP	⭕	IDP or UK/EU licence + certified translation required
Insurance: Green Card	⭕	Take out local insurance at border
DRL	✅	Recommended
Mobile phones	❌	Not recommended (information not available)
Radar detectors		
GPS speed camera alerts (POI)	❌	Not recommended (information not available)
Emergency services	112	
i	dyp.gov.az/?/en/mainpage/	

DRIVING EQUIPMENT		
Warning triangle	⭕	Required (inside car)
High-vis jacket(s)	✅	Recommended
First-aid kit	⭕	Required (inside car)
Fire extinguisher	⭕	Required (inside car)
Spare bulbs	✅	Recommended
Spare fuel (can)	✅	Allowed
Winter tyres	✅	Recommended in wintry conditions
Snow chains		
Additional items	⭕	Nationality sticker (even with Euro-style number plate) Carnet de Passage en Douane recommended

TOLLS	
🚧 No toll roads	

Belarus

D riving in Belarus and Russia (see page 136) is very similar, with many shared road signs and regulations. The police carry out regular checks on foreign-registered cars, and can issue on-the-spot fines.

Here, too, it's a good idea to obtain an International Certificate for Motor Vehicles (ICMV) before you go. You may import a car temporarily for up to three months. Be wary of offers of help with border formalities from private individuals.

Diesel ('Solyarka') and LPG are generally available, and credit cards are accepted in many filling stations. Check with your card issuer before you travel, however, as some foreign cards may not be accepted.

Blind pedestrians present

Crawler lane; minimum speed in main lanes

SPEED LIMITS				km/h
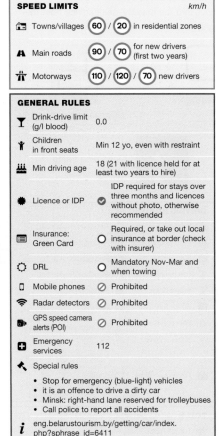 Towns/villages	60 / 20	in residential zones		
Main roads	90 / 70	for new drivers (first two years)		
Motorways	110 / 120 / 70	new drivers		

End of priority road

Except cars (applied to restriction)

GENERAL RULES	
Drink-drive limit (g/l blood)	0.0
Children in front seats	Min 12 yo, even with restraint
Min driving age	18 (21 with licence held for at least two years to hire)
Licence or IDP	IDP required for stays over three months and licences without photo, otherwise recommended
Insurance: Green Card	Required, or take out local insurance at border (check with insurer)
DRL	Mandatory Nov-Mar and when towing
Mobile phones	Prohibited
Radar detectors	Prohibited
GPS speed camera alerts (POI)	Prohibited
Emergency services	112
Special rules	• Stop for emergency (blue-light) vehicles • it is an offence to drive a dirty car • Minsk: right-hand lane reserved for trolleybuses • Call police to report all accidents
i	eng.belarustourism.by/getting/car/index.php?sphrase_id=6411

DRIVING EQUIPMENT		
Warning triangle	○	Required (inside car)
High-vis jacket(s)	○	Required
First-aid kit	○	Required
Fire extinguisher	○	Required
Spare bulbs	◉	Recommended
Spare fuel (can)	◉	Allowed (max 20L): declare on entry
Winter tyres	○	Winter tyres mandatory mid-Nov to mid-Mar
Snow chains		
Additional items	○	Nationality sticker (even with Euro-style number plate), ICMV recommended

TOLLS	
Tolls on some sections, inc M1/E30 highway	
How to pay	On-board unit (tag) available at borders and major filling stations
i	www.beltoll.by
Road tax levied at border	

Bosnia-Herzegovina

I f you've the misfortune to break down in Bosnia-Herzegovina, try to do so in a German make of car! Secondhand German cars, including Volkswagen and Mercedes, are well represented on Bosnia-Herzegovina's roads, so spare parts are easier to find. If you drive a car built in another country, carrying some basic spares is a good safeguard.

Road conditions are steadily improving, but the country has many twisty mountain roads: you should give way to vehicles coming uphill, and reckon on a modest average speed. Like many countries in Central and Eastern Europe, Bosnia-Herzegovina takes drink-driving, especially for young drivers, very seriously. As well as imposing a zero alcohol limit for new drivers, from 2300-0500 drivers under 23 must be accompanied by another adult driver. To avoid the risk of distracting the driver, visibly intoxicated passengers may not travel in the front seat of any car.

If you commit a traffic offence, the police can issue a ticket on-the-spot, but fines are payable at banks or post offices, normally within eight days, and you should obtain an official receipt, which you may need to show when you leave the country.

SPEED LIMITS

		km/h
🚗	Towns/villages	(50)
🛣	Main roads	(80) / (100) (dual carriageways)
🏍	Motorways	(130)

GENERAL RULES

🍷	Drink-drive limit (g/l blood)	0.3; 0.0 for new drivers (under 21/first three years)
🧒	Children in front seats	Min 12 yo, even with restraint
👥	Min driving age	18
✳	Licence or IDP	✓ IDP required for licences without photo, otherwise recommended
🪪	Insurance: Green Card	◯ Required or take out local insurance at border (check with insurer)
☼	DRL	◯ Required; dipped headlights preferred
📱	Mobile phones	⊘ Handheld phones prohibited ⊗ Hands-free tolerated, but not recommended
📶	Radar detectors	⊘ Prohibited
📡	GPS speed camera alerts (POI)	⊘ Prohibited
➕	Emergency services	112
🔧	Special rules	• Clear all snow and ice from car in winter • Call police to report all accidents
i	www.bhtourism.ba/eng/bycar.wbsp	

DRIVING EQUIPMENT

⚠	Warning triangle	◯ Required (inside car); two if towing
🦺	High-vis jacket(s)	◯ Required for all passengers (inside car)
🧰	First-aid kit	◯ Required
🧯	Fire extinguisher	◯ Required for LPG vehicles; otherwise recommended
💡	Spare bulbs	◯ Required
⛽	Spare fuel (can)	✓ Allowed
⚙	Winter tyres	◯ Mandatory (min 4mm tread depth) on driven wheels 15 Nov-15 Apr
❄	Snow chains	◯ Use chains when indicated by signs
🧳	Additional items	◯ Tow rope Jack and spare wheel or repair kit Nationality sticker (even with Euro-style number plate)

TOLLS

🏍	Toll on A1 motorway	
🎫	How to pay	Cash (inc euros) or tag (ACC)
i	www.jpautoceste.ba/en/	

Bulgaria

With its ski stations and Black Sea resorts, Bulgaria is gradually opening up to visiting motorists. Its motorways (signposted in green) are generally well surfaced, and signs are in both Cyrillic and Roman script. Other roads, however, can be in poor condition or suffer landslides.

In the Blue and Green parking zones in towns, rather than use a parking disc, you buy a ticket from a kiosk or seller on the street and write your arrival time on that. Overnight, however, it is recommended to leave your car in a secure, guarded car park. Many filling stations only accept cash.

There have been reports of bogus police and border officials: if you have any doubts, ask to see their ID, and get an official receipt for any fines.

Bulgaria

SPEED LIMITS
km/h

🏠	Towns/villages	**50**
🛣	Main roads	**90**
🛣	Motorways	**120** to **140** (as signed)

GENERAL RULES

⊤	Drink-drive limit (g/l blood)	0.0
👶	Children in front seats	Min 12 yo and 1.5m height, even with restraint
👥	Min driving age	18 (21-25 with licence held for at least one year to hire)
✳	Licence or IDP	✓ IDP required for licences without photo, otherwise recommended
📇	Insurance: Green Card	◯ Required
☼	DRL	◯ Required; dipped headlights preferred
☐	Mobile phones	⊘ Handheld phones prohibited / ✕ Hands-free tolerated, but not recommended
📶	Radar detectors	⊘ Prohibited
🔛	GPS speed camera alerts (POI)	NA (no fixed cameras)
➕	Emergency services	112
🔧	Special rules	

- Priority to the right: give way to vehicles approaching from the right (unless signs indicate otherwise)
- Eating & smoking at wheel prohibited
- Forbidden to drive wearing high heels, flip-flops or dark sunglasses
- Forbidden to use horn at night and only to avoid accidents by day

i www.mvr.bg/en/

DRIVING EQUIPMENT

⚠	Warning triangle	◯ Required
🦺	High-vis jacket(s)	◯ Required for all passengers
🧰	First-aid kit	◯ Required
🧯	Fire extinguisher	◯ Required for cars registered in country; recommended for visitors
💡	Spare bulbs	✓ Recommended
⛽	Spare fuel (can)	⊘ Prohibited
❄	Winter tyres	✓ Mandatory for cars registered in country; recommended for visitors
❄	Snow chains	◯ Chains must be carried 1 Nov-1 Mar
🧳	Additional items	◯ Jack, wheel wrench and spare wheel or repair kit Recommended: inventory of caravan/trailer contents Nationality sticker (even with Euro-style number plate)

TOLLS

🛣	Road Tax: Vinetka/vignette (sticker) to use all roads	
💳	How to pay	Available for one week/one month/one year, covers car and trailer Buy at borders, post offices, service stations, Piccadilly supermarkets and online

i www.vinetka.com

🚗 Some bridge crossings over Danube

Croatia

C roatia is popular with tourists, and traffic can be heavy in summer. Its main roads are well maintained, and most major filling stations take credit cards. Watch out though for ticket touts selling bogus toll tickets on some motorways. In Zagreb, zones coded with different colours (red, yellow, then green) allow progressively longer stays as you move out from the centre. For speeding and other offences, the police can impose on-the-spot fines, which must be paid at once, or at a bank or post office within eight days.

SPEED LIMITS
km/h

Towns/villages	**50**	
Main roads	**90** / **110** (**80** / **100**	new drivers under 25)
M'ways	**130** (**120** new drivers)	

GENERAL RULES

Drink-drive limit (g/l blood)	0.5; 0.0 for new drivers	
Children in front seats	Min 12 yo, even with restraint	
Min driving age	18 (21 with licence held for at least one year to hire)	
Licence or IDP	✓	IDP required to hire car and recommended for non-EU licences; otherwise UK photocard or three-part pink licence recommended
Insurance: Green Card	✓	Recommended: must specify Croatia and Bosnia-Herzegovina to use Dalmatian Coastal Highway
DRL	O	Required in winter (when clocks change)
Mobile phones	⊘	Handheld phones prohibited
	✖	Hands-free tolerated, but not recommended
Radar detectors	⊘	Prohibited
GPS speed camera alerts (POI)	✓	Allowed
Emergency services	112	
Special rules		

- Existing damage to car must be certified on entry
- Priority to the right: give way to vehicles approaching from the right (unless signs indicate otherwise)
- Cars entering roundabout have priority
- Buses have right of way
- Call police to report all accidents

i croatia.hr/en-GB/Journey-through-Croatia
www.hak.hr (traffic info)

Electronic toll

Tunnel (with length)

Hospital

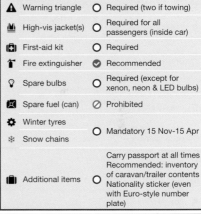
Stop – wrong way

DRIVING EQUIPMENT

⚠	Warning triangle	O	Required (two if towing)
🦺	High-vis jacket(s)	O	Required for all passengers (inside car)
🧰	First-aid kit	O	Required
🧯	Fire extinguisher	✓	Recommended
💡	Spare bulbs	O	Required (except for xenon, neon & LED bulbs)
🛢	Spare fuel (can)	⊘	Prohibited
❄	Winter tyres		
❄	Snow chains	O	Mandatory 15 Nov-15 Apr
🧳	Additional items	O	Carry passport at all times Recommended: inventory of caravan/trailer contents Nationality sticker (even with Euro-style number plate)

TOLLS

🛣	Tolls on most motorways
🚘	How to pay Cash/credit card/tag (ETC)
i	www.hac.hr/en/
🔲	Various bridges & tunnels, inc. Krk Bridge & Ucka Tunnel

Czech Republic

One of the easiest countries in Central Europe to reach from the UK, France or Germany, the Czech Republic has a good motorway network, and many rules are similar to those in Germany. If traffic backs up, you must create a free lane between the lines of traffic to allow emergency vehicles to get through. When two lanes of traffic merge into one, use the 'zipper' principle and filter in turn. The police can collect on-the-spot fines, and retain visitors' driving licences for serious offences. They should be called to any accidents involving injury or serious damage, or if vehicles block the road.

SPEED LIMITS   km/h

🏠	Towns/ villages	**50** / **20** in residential zones
A	Main roads	**90**
🛣	M'ways	**130** / **80** in built-up areas

Fog

Winter tyres required

GENERAL RULES

🍸	Drink-drive limit (g/l blood)	0.0
🧒	Children in front seats	Min 12 yo, 1.5m height and 36kg, unless suitable restraint used
👥	Min driving age	18 (21 with licence held for at least one year to hire)
✳	Licence or IDP	✅ IDP required for licences without photo and stays over three months
📰	Insurance: Green Card	✅ Recommended
◯	DRL	◯ Required
📱	Mobile phones	⊘ Handheld phones prohibited ❌ Hands-free tolerated, but not recommended
📶	Radar detectors	⊘ Prohibited
📷	GPS speed camera alerts (POI)	✅ Allowed
➕	Emergency services	112
🔧	Special rules	

- Existing damage to car must be certified on entry
- Priority to the right: give way to vehicles approaching from the right (unless signs indicate otherwise)
- Speed limit 30km/h for 50m before level crossings

i www.ibesip.cz/en/road-safety/road-safety-rules-in-the-czech-republic

DRIVING EQUIPMENT

⚠	Warning triangle	◯ Required
🦺	High-vis jacket(s)	◯ Required for all passengers (inside car)
🧰	First-aid kit	◯ Required (check contents with local pharmacy)
🧯	Fire extinguisher	✅ Recommended
💡	Spare bulbs	◯ Required (except for xenon, neon & LED bulbs)
⛽	Spare fuel (can)	✅ Allowed (max 10L)
⚙	Winter tyres	◯ Mandatory (4mm min tread depth) 1 Nov-3 Mar and at all times under 4°C
❄	Snow chains	Approved socks may be used as alternative to chains (as signed)
🧳	Additional items	◯ Jack and spare wheel or repair kit Replacement fuses Recommended: inventory of caravan/trailer contents

TOLLS

🛣 Tolls on nearly all motorways

🪪	How to pay	Vignette (sticker) available for ten days/one month/one year Buy at borders, from post offices and service stations

i www.motorway.cz

Estonia

Estonia has much unspoilt countryside, but watch out for moose or deer on the road, especially at dusk, and be ready to pull over to the hard shoulder to let faster vehicles overtake. Winters can be severe, but the local authorities take advantage of these conditions by creating temporary ice roads across some lakes and rivers. Specially formulated winter diesel is sold, and most filling stations take credit cards.

Keep a close eye on your speed, as there is a very narrow margin before fines are imposed. Speeding and parking fines can be high, but cities such as Tallinn have modern, mobile phone-based payment schemes in authorised parking areas. Unfortunately, there are some instances of car crime, so leave your car in a guarded car park overnight if you can.

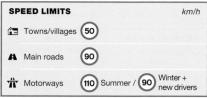

SPEED LIMITS		km/h
Towns/villages	**50**	
Main roads	**90**	
Motorways	**110** Summer / **90**	Winter + new drivers

GENERAL RULES	
Drink-drive limit (g/l blood)	0.2
Children in front seats	Min 12 yo and 1.35m height, unless suitable restraint used
Min driving age	18 (20-25 to hire)
Licence or IDP	✅ UK photocard or three-part pink licence required; otherwise IDP recommended
Insurance: Green Card	✅ Recommended
DRL	⭕ Required; dipped headlights preferred
Mobile phones	⊘ Handheld phones prohibited
	✖ Hands-free tolerated, but not recommended
Radar detectors GPS speed camera alerts (POI)	⊘ Prohibited
Emergency services	112
Special rules	• Priority to the right: give way to vehicles approaching from the right (unless signs indicate otherwise) • Give way to pedestrians at unregulated crossroads • Do not overtake trams at stops • Keep number plates clean • Call police if accidents involve injuries or if road blocked
i	www.politsei.ee/en/nouanded/liiklus/

Tarmac road ends

DRIVING EQUIPMENT		
⚠ Warning triangle	⭕	Two required
High-vis jacket(s)	⭕	Required for driver; recommended for all passengers
First-aid kit	⭕	Required
Fire extinguisher	✅	Recommended
Spare bulbs	✅	Recommended
Spare fuel (can)	✅	Allowed (max 10L duty-free)
Winter tyres	⭕	Winter tyres mandatory (3mm min tread depth) 1 Dec-1 Mar (or longer if weather dictates)
Snow chains		
Additional items	⭕	Jack, 2x wheel chocks, and torch Vehicles towing trailer must have exterior mirrors on both sides

TOLLS	
Free
To enter Tallinn

Estonia

Georgia

At the crossroads of Europe and Asia, Georgia is a member of the Council of Europe. It's a long trip by road from Western Europe, and definitely one that should be reserved for intrepid – and experienced – travellers. Tensions with Russia have remained high over the past decade: take advice from the government in your country before travelling. At the time of going to press, the British Foreign & Commonwealth Office advises against entering or leaving Georgia by road from Russia. The M27 road (also known as the M1) should also be avoided, due to the risk of criminal activity. See www.gov.uk/foreign-travel-advice for the latest guidance.

Although there are express roads towards Russia, and, in the south, to the neighbouring countries of Armenia, Azerbaijan and Turkey, roads are generally in poor condition. White lines are often missing and damage is common, especially after heavy rain. Local drivers may seem reckless; driving at night can be especially dangerous, so avoid this if you can. In the capital, Tbilisi, there are colour-coded parking zones, but it's advisable to leave your car in a secure car park and to take a licensed taxi.

SPEED LIMITS		km/h
🚗 Towns/villages	(30) to (60)	(as signed)
🅰 Main roads	(80) / (100)	
🛣 Motorways	(80) / (110)	

GENERAL RULES		
🍷 Drink-drive limit (g/l blood)	0.0	
🧍 Children in front seats	Min 12 yo, even with restraint	
👥 Min driving age	18 (check with agency for car hire)	
✳ Licence or IDP	⭕ IDP required for car hire, otherwise strongly recommended	
📇 Insurance: Green Card	⭕ Required	
💡 DRL	✅ Recommended	
📱 Mobile phones	🚫 Prohibited	
📡 Radar detectors	🚫 Prohibited	
📟 GPS speed camera alerts (POI)	❌ Not recommended (information not available)	
➕ Emergency services	112	

DRIVING EQUIPMENT		
⚠ Warning triangle	⭕ Required (inside car)	
🦺 High-vis jacket(s)	✅ Recommended	
🧰 First-aid kit	⭕ Required	
🧯 Fire extinguisher	⭕ Required	
💡 Spare bulbs	✅ Recommended	
⛽ Spare fuel (can)	❌ Not recommended (information not available)	
⚙ Winter tyres ❄ Snow chains	⭕ Chains required on some roads out of Tbilisi and on Choloki & Rikoti Passes	
🧳 Additional items	⭕ Nationality sticker (even with Euro-style number plate) Carnet de Passage en Douane recommended	

TOLLS	
🛣 Free	

Variable speed limits by lane

For taxis

Contraflow: change carriageways

Height restriction (3.5m)

Hungary

Although winters can be harsh, Hungary's roads are generally well maintained. On motorways, as in neighbouring Austria, you should leave a free lane to allow emergency vehicles to get through queuing traffic. The police can issue on-the-spot fines, which can be paid at banks or post offices. There is a strict zero alcohol rule when driving.

In built-up areas, yellow zigzag lines indicate parking restrictions, with tickets available for up to two hours' parking in authorised spaces. Pollution is becoming an issue in Budapest, with restrictions applied on high-pollution days.

SPEED LIMITS
km/h

🏘 Towns/villages	**50** / **30**	in some areas
🛣 Main roads	**90** / **110**	dual carriageways
🛣 Motorways	**130**	

GENERAL RULES

🍸 Drink-drive limit (g/l blood)	0.0	
🧍 Children in front seats	Min 12 yo and 1.5m height, unless suitable restraint used	
👥 Min driving age	18 (21 with licence held for at least one year to hire)	
✳ Licence or IDP	✓	UK photocard or three-part pink licence required; otherwise IDP recommended
🗎 Insurance: Green Card	✓	Recommended
☼ DRL	○	Required outside built-up areas; dipped headlights preferred
📱 Mobile phones	⊘	Handheld phones prohibited
	✕	Hands-free tolerated, but not recommended
📡 Radar detectors	⊘	Prohibited
GPS speed camera alerts (POI)	✓	Allowed
➕ Emergency services	112	
🔧 Special rules		

- Priority to the right: give way to vehicles approaching from the right (unless signs indicate otherwise)
- Give way to trams & buses
- Forbidden to use horn in built-up areas, except in immediate danger
- No parking on bridges or in front of public buildings

You will usually need cash to buy fuel. If your car breaks down, you can call the Hungarian Autóklub's English-language breakdown service on +36 13 45 17 55.

Toll station

Accident ahead

DRIVING EQUIPMENT

⚠ Warning triangle	○	Required (inside car)
🦺 High-vis jacket(s)	○	Required for all passengers (inside car): all pedestrians must wear reflective clothing at night
🧰 First-aid kit	○	Required
🧯 Fire extinguisher	✓	Recommended
💡 Spare bulbs	○	Required (except for xenon, neon & LED bulbs)
⛽ Spare fuel (can)	⊘	Prohibited
⚙ Winter tyres	✓	Recommended in wintry conditions
❄ Snow chains	○	Use as signed
🧳 Additional items	✓	Recommended: tow rope, inventory of caravan/trailer contents

TOLLS

🛣	Tolls on most motorways	
💳 How to pay		Electronic vignette Covers car and trailer Available for ten days/one month/one year Buy at borders and from service stations
ℹ	www.toll-charge.hu	

Kosovo

War has left a sad mark on Kosovo, and travellers visiting it by car need to take special care. There have been cases of damage to foreign-registered hire cars, so check with your rental company if you plan to enter Kosovo with a hire car registered in Albania, Bulgaria or Serbia. The British Foreign & Commonwealth Office advises against using some of the border crossings, with long queues possible at other entry points. See www.gov.uk/foreign-travel-advice for current information, and on occasional violence in areas including Mitrovica.

All roads have now been cleared of mines, but away from them, unexploded devices may remain, so do not attempt to go off-road. Many roads are in poor condition, especially in rural areas or following bad weather. Local driving standards, especially in Pristina, leave much to be desired, with aggressive driving common.

SPEED LIMITS		*km/h*
🚗 Towns/villages	**50**	
🏍 Main roads	**80** / **110**	dual carriageways
🏛 Motorways	**130**	

GENERAL RULES

🍷 Drink-drive limit (g/l blood)	0.5	
🧍 Children in front seats	Min 12 yo, even with restraint	
👥 Min driving age	18 (21 to hire)	
✵ Licence or IDP	✅	IDP required for non-EU licences, otherwise recommended
▭ Insurance: Green Card	❌	Green Card not accepted, take out local insurance at border
☼ DRL	⭕	Required
📱 Mobile phones	⊘	Handheld phones prohibited
	❌	Hands-free tolerated, but not recommended
📶 Radar detectors		Not recommended
📷 GPS speed camera alerts (POI)	❌	(information not available)
➕ Emergency services		Police 92 (192 from mobile) Ambulance 94 Fire 93
🔧 Special rules		

- Priority to the right: give way to vehicles approaching from the right (unless signs indicate otherwise)
- Driver may not get out of car with engine running
- Visibly intoxicated passengers may not travel in front seat
- Call police to report all accidents

A wintry road in Kosovo.
(Courtesy Katarzyna Mazurowska/Thinkstock)

DRIVING EQUIPMENT

⚠ Warning triangle	⭕	Required (inside car; two if towing)
🦺 High-vis jacket(s)	⭕	Required for all passengers (inside car)
🧰 First-aid kit	⭕	Required
🧯 Fire extinguisher	✅	Recommended
💡 Spare bulbs	✅	Recommended
⛽ Spare fuel (can)	✅	Allowed (max 10L)
⚙ Winter tyres	⭕	Winter tyres (min 4mm tread depth), or snow chains, mandatory on driven wheels 1 Nov- 1 Apr
❄ Snow chains		
🧳 Additional items	⭕	Spare wheel or repair kit, tow rope Nationality sticker (even with Euro-style number plate)

TOLLS

🏛 Free

Latvia

O ver the past decade, Latvia's accident rate has seen major improvements and then slipped back again, but the authorities are committed to making it a safer place to travel in. Its road network is largely in good condition, although some rural roads are unsurfaced and can be dusty in summer. Winter often brings snow and icy conditions, but special winter diesel is available to cope with severe cold. Most petrol stations accept credit cards.

Riga Tweed Run on the streets of the Old Town. (Courtesy imantsu/Thinkstock)

As in Estonia, it's customary to use the hard shoulder on single-carriageway roads to let faster cars overtake. In rural areas, especially at night, watch out for unlit farm vehicles. If you are unlucky enough to have an accident, these should always be reported to the police, and you should wait for their permission before moving your vehicle. The police can impose on-the-spot fines.

Riga is a young and vibrant capital, with an interesting motor museum well worth visiting by car enthusiasts. Unfortunately, there is also some car crime, so use guarded car parks whenever you can.

SPEED LIMITS

		km/h
Towns/villages	(50) / (20)	in residential zones
Main roads	(90)	Motorways (110)

GENERAL RULES

Drink-drive limit (g/l blood)	0.5; 0.2 for new drivers (first two years)	
Children in front seats	Min 12 yo and 1.5m height, unless suitable restraint used	
Min driving age	18 (21-25 with licence held for at least two years to hire)	
Licence or IDP	✓	UK photocard or three-part pink licence recommended; otherwise IDP recommended
Insurance: Green Card	✓	Recommended
DRL	O	Required; dipped headlights preferred
Mobile phones	⊘	Handheld phones prohibited
	✗	Hands-free tolerated, but not recommended
Radar detectors	⊘	Prohibited
GPS speed camera alerts (POI)	✓	Allowed
Emergency services	112	
Special rules		
• Priority to the right: give way to vehicles approaching from the right (unless signs indicate otherwise)		
i www.csdd.lv/eng		

DRIVING EQUIPMENT

⚠	Warning triangle	O	Two required
🦺	High-vis jacket(s)	O	Required for all passengers (inside car): all pedestrians must wear reflective clothing at night
🧰	First-aid kit	O	Required
🧯	Fire extinguisher	O	Required for cars registered in country; recommended for visitors
💡	Spare bulbs	✓	Recommended
⛽	Spare fuel (can)	✓	Allowed (max 20L), duty payable
❄	Winter tyres	O	Winter tyres mandatory (min 3mm tread depth) 1 Dec-1 Apr (and beyond if conditions dictate)
❄	Snow chains		
🧳	Additional items	O	Nationality sticker (even with Euro-style number plate)

TOLLS

🛣 Free	
🎫 To enter Jurmala	

Latvia

Lithuania

With its attractive coastal roads, lakes and forests, Lithuania is a little known, but pleasant country to tour by car. Its motorways are free, but can be used by pedestrians, cycles and horse-drawn carts, as well as fast-moving cars, so take extra care, especially when your view ahead is limited.

Temperatures in winter can be very low, and winter driving requires extra attention, with lower speed limits on motorways (see Checklist below). Reduced speed limits also apply in residential zones and car parks, and on gravel rather than asphalt roads. There are on-the-spot fines for even the smallest speeding offences. As in many countries in northern Europe, the winter diesel available locally will continue to work at much lower temperatures than the fuel sold in milder countries. Most filling stations accept major credit cards. It's worthwhile carrying some basic spares with you, as parts for some cars may be hard to obtain at short notice in Lithuania.

If you are staying in the capital, Vilnius, it's recommended to leave your car in a secure, guarded car park overnight.

SPEED LIMITS

km/h

Towns/villages	50	/ 20	residential zones & car parks	
Main roads	70	gravel roads /	90	asphalt
M'ways	110	Nov-Mar	130	Apr-Oct

GENERAL RULES

Drink-drive limit (g/l blood)	0.4; 0.0 for new drivers (first two years)
Children in front seats	Min 12 yo and 1.35m height, unless suitable restraint used
Min driving age	18 (21-25 to hire)
Licence or IDP	✓ UK photocard or three-part pink licence recommended; otherwise IDP recommended
Insurance: Green Card	✓ Recommended
DRL	○ Required; dipped headlights preferred
Mobile phones	⊘ Handheld phones prohibited
	✗ Hands-free tolerated, but not recommended
Radar detectors	⊘ Prohibited
GPS speed camera alerts (POI)	✗ Not recommended (law unclear)
Emergency services	112
Special rules	

- On single-carriageway roads, use hard shoulder to let faster cars overtake
- At junctions with red light and green filter arrow to turn, stop before turning
- No parking within 15m of bus stop or 5m of crossroads
- Do not carry opened bottles of alcohol in car
- Call police to accidents involving injuries or disputed responsibility

i www.lietuva.lt/en/tourism/travelling_tips/useful_information

DRIVING EQUIPMENT

⚠ Warning triangle	○	Required
High-vis jacket(s)	○	Required for all passengers (inside car): all pedestrians must wear reflective clothing at night
First-aid kit	○	Required
Fire extinguisher	○	Required for cars registered in country; recommended for visitors
Spare bulbs	✓	Recommended
Spare fuel (can)	✓	Allowed (max 10L), duty payable
Winter tyres	○	Winter tyres mandatory 10 Nov-1 Apr
Snow chains		
Additional items	○	Nationality sticker (even with Euro-style number plate)

TOLLS

M'ways	Free

Macedonia (FYROM)

ts government is determined to make Macedonia's roads safer, but excessive speed by local drivers, and poorly made, twisty roads have contributed to its unenviable record. In winter, heavy fog around Skopje often adds to the dangers faced by motorists.

Be prepared for long queues in the summer, especially at the Tabanovce border crossing with Serbia. If your car has any existing damage, this should be declared on entry to the country, as should any damage you incur if you have an accident whilst in Macedonia.

The police can issue on-the-spot fines, but these should be paid at a bank or post office, where you'll be given a receipt. Not all filling stations take credit cards.

SPEED LIMITS (km/h)

🏠 Towns/villages	(50)	
🅰 Main roads	(80) / (100)	dual carriageways
🛣 Motorways	(120) / (130)	

GENERAL RULES

🍷 Drink-drive limit (g/l blood)	0.5; 0.0 for new drivers (first two years)	
🧍 Children in front seats	Min 12 yo, even with restraint	
👥 Min driving age	18 (21-23 with licence for at least two years to hire); see Special rules	
✳ Licence or IDP	✅ IDP recommended	
📧 Insurance: Green Card	⭕ Required	
☼ DRL	⭕ Required; dipped headlights preferred	
📱 Mobile phones	⊘ Handheld phones prohibited	
	✖ Hands-free tolerated, but not recommended	
📶 Radar detectors	⊘ Prohibited	
📷 GPS speed camera alerts (POI)	✅ Allowed	
➕ Emergency services	112	
🔧 Special rules		

- Priority to the right: give way to vehicles approaching from the right (unless signs indicate otherwise)
- New drivers (under 25) may not drive from 2300-0500 unless accompanied by adult driver over 25
- Visibly intoxicated passengers may not travel in front seat

Manual traffic control ahead

Switch off engine

DRIVING EQUIPMENT

🅰 Warning triangle	⭕ Required (two if towing)	
👷 High-vis jacket(s)	⭕ Required for all passengers (inside car)	
🧰 First-aid kit	⭕ Required	
🧯 Fire extinguisher	⭕ Required for LPG-powered cars, otherwise recommended	
💡 Spare bulbs	⭕ Required (except for xenon, neon & LED bulbs)	
⛽ Spare fuel (can)	✅ Allowed (max 20L duty free)	
⚙ Winter tyres	⭕ Winter tyres mandatory (min 4mm tread depth) on all four wheels 15 Nov-15 Mar,	
❄ Snow chains	⭕ Use snow chains as signed	
🎒 Additional items	⭕ Tow rope Nationality sticker (even with Euro-style number plate)	

TOLLS

🛣 Tolls on motorways		
💳 How to pay	Cash (Macedonian denars), credit cards not always accepted	

Moldova

Moldova

At night in Chisinau. (Courtesy UmbertoPantalone/ Thinkstock)

Most visits to Moldova by foreigners are trouble-free, although there is some petty crime in Chisinau. If you are driving into Moldova, however, you should pay close attention to the entry requirements. If you're coming from Ukraine, you should avoid entering Moldova through Transnistria: there are no official controls and you may have difficulty leaving Moldova later, without any proof that you entered the country officially. For UK citizens, see the FCO website at www.gov.uk/foreign-travel-advice for more details. A Green Card has normally been required as proof of insurance for all foreign vehicles, but an additional, local insurance requirement in Transnistria is due to be introduced from 2016. The Moldovan authorities take firm action against all visitors who overstay the term of their visas, and foreign-registered vehicles may only be imported for a maximum of 90 days.

Once through the border crossing, driving conditions in Moldova are similar to those in many countries on the Eastern edge of Europe. More than 80% of Moldova's roads are laid with asphalt, but some are of poor quality. Credit cards may not be accepted at filling stations away from major cities.

SPEED LIMITS			km/h
🚗 Towns/villages	(50) / (20)	residential zones	
🛣 Main roads	(80)		

GENERAL RULES	
Ⴢ Drink-drive limit (g/l blood)	0.0
Ⴕ Children in front seats	Min 12 yo, even with restraint
👥 Min driving age	18 (21-23 to hire car)
✳ Licence or IDP	✅ IDP recommended
📇 Insurance: Green Card	⭕ Required; see main text
⚙ DRL	⭕ Required Nov-Mar; dipped headlights preferred
📱 Mobile phones	❌ Not recommended (information not available)
📶 Radar detectors	
🚓 GPS speed camera alerts (POI)	❌ Not recommended (information not available)
➕ Emergency services	112
🔧 Special rules	• Call police within two hours of any accident

DRIVING EQUIPMENT		
🔺 Warning triangle	⭕	Required
🦺 High-vis jacket(s)	⭕	Required
🧰 First-aid kit	⭕	Required
🧯 Fire extinguisher	⭕	Required
💡 Spare bulbs	✅	Recommended
⛽ Spare fuel (can)	⊘	Prohibited
⚙ Winter tyres	⭕	Required in wintry conditions
❄ Snow chains		
🧳 Additional items	⭕	Nationality sticker (even with Euro-style number plate)

TOLLS	
⛎ Road tax to use all roads	
💳 How to pay	Payable at border on entry Available for seven/15/30/90/180 days

Montenegro

Montenegro's scenic mountain roads were once special stages for international competitions like the 1970 World Cup Rally and are now being re-discovered by motoring enthusiasts from abroad. Beautiful as they are, they demand care: rock falls are frequent and crash barriers are not always well maintained.

Driving at night can be especially hazardous, and many passes are closed altogether in winter. Over half of Montenegro's roads are fully surfaced, but elsewhere a four-wheel drive will make a good choice. LPG is generally available, and many filling stations accept credit cards.

As in Macedonia, you should get any existing damage to your car certified when you enter the country. Call the police for all accidents involving injury and ensure that any damage to your car is recorded. The police may issue on-the-spot fines, but do not collect payment.

SPEED LIMITS _km/h_

🏘	Towns/villages	**50**
🛣	Main roads	**80** / **100**
🛣	Motorways	**120**

GENERAL RULES

🍷	Drink-drive limit (g/l blood)	0.3
🧒	Children in front seats	Min 12 yo, even with restraint
👥	Min driving age	18 (23 to hire)
✴	Licence or IDP	✅ IDP recommended
▤	Insurance: Green Card	⭘ Required (must specify Montenegro)
☼	DRL	⭘ Required; dipped headlights preferred
📱	Mobile phones	⊘ Handheld phones prohibited
		❌ Hands-free tolerated, but not recommended
📶	Radar detectors	
📷	GPS speed camera alerts (POI)	❌ Not recommended (information not available)
➕	Emergency services	112
🔧	Special rules	

- Indicate throughout overtaking manoeuvres
- Vehicles entering roundabout have priority
- Do not overtake school buses at stop
- Do not use horn in towns, except in immediate danger
- Flip-flops may not be worn when driving
- Visibly intoxicated passengers may not travel in front seat

Exploring Montenegro's mountain roads.
(Courtesy supergenijalac/Thinkstock)

DRIVING EQUIPMENT

⚠	Warning triangle	⭘ Required (two if towing)
🦺	High-vis jacket(s)	⭘ Required (inside car)
🧰	First-aid kit	⭘ Required
🧯	Fire extinguisher	✅ Recommended
💡	Spare bulbs	⭘ Required
⛽	Spare fuel (can)	✅ Allowed
❄	Winter tyres	⭘ Winter tyres mandatory on driven wheels 15 Nov- 31 Mar
❄	Snow chains	
🧳	Additional items	⭘ Carry passport at all times Nationality sticker (even with Euro-style number plate) Snow shovel recommended in winter

TOLLS

🛣	Free	
🚇	Sozina Tunnel	
💳	How to pay	Cash

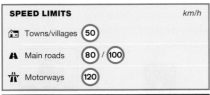

Montenegro

Poland

Traffic conditions are often hazardous on Poland's crowded roads, and it has one of the worst accident rates in Europe. Look out especially for drivers around you who use headlights to indicate that they're overtaking. The police should be called to all accidents. Outside towns, traffic police must be in uniform and show their ID. They can issue on-the-spot fines, which foreign visitors must settle immediately in cash.

The motorway network is being expanded, but there are many roadworks, causing frequent and time-consuming diversions. Older roads can be in poor repair, with ruts often forming.

In cities, look for signs showing secure 24-hour parking ('Strzeżony – 24H'). LPG is widely available, and credit cards are normally accepted.

Change of priority at junction

Ruts

SPEED LIMITS		km/h
🏘 Towns/villages	50 / 60	2300-0500 hours
🛣 Main roads	90 / 100	dual carriageways
🛤 Motorways	120 to 140	as signed

GENERAL RULES	
Drink-drive limit (g/l blood)	0.2 (also cyclists)
Children in front seats	Min 12 yo and 1.5m height, unless suitable restraint used
Min driving age	18 (21-25 with licence held for at least one year to hire)
Licence or IDP	✓ UK photocard or three-part pink licence required; otherwise IDP recommended
Insurance: Green Card	✓ Recommended
DRL	O Required; dipped headlights preferred
Mobile phones	⊘ Handheld phones prohibited
	✗ Hands-free tolerated, but not recommended
Radar detectors	⊘ Prohibited
GPS speed camera alerts (POI)	✓ Allowed
Emergency services	112
Special rules	

- Priority to the right: give way to vehicles approaching from the right (unless signs indicate otherwise)
- Traffic on roundabout has priority (unless signs indicate otherwise)
- At junctions with red light and green filter arrow to turn, stop before turning
- Trams & buses have priority
- Do not use horn in towns, except in immediate danger

i www.poland.travel/en-gb/travel-by-car/road-traffic-regulations

DRIVING EQUIPMENT		
⚠ Warning triangle	O	Required
🦺 High-vis jacket(s)	O	Required for all passengers for cars registered in country; recommended for visitors
🧰 First-aid kit	O	Required
🧯 Fire extinguisher	O	Required for cars registered in country; recommended for visitors
💡 Spare bulbs	✓	Recommended
⛽ Spare fuel (can)	⚠	Allowed (max 10L); prohibited on ferries
⚙ Winter tyres	✓	Recommended
❄ Snow chains	O	Use as signed
🧳 Additional items	O	For cars registered in country: anti-theft device and rear mud flaps

TOLLS	
🛤	Tolls on many motorways (inc A1, A2 & A4)
💳 How to pay	Cash or (pre-paid) tag
i	www.viatoll.pl

Romania

When the BBC TV programme *Top Gear* named the Transfăgărăşan Highway "the best road in the world," Romania's mountain passes found unexpected fame, and now attract large numbers of tourists in summer.

New motorways are being built, but elsewhere, driving in Romania can feel like stepping back in time. Signposting is sometimes inadequate, so plan your route carefully, and look out for reckless local drivers.

The police should be called to all accidents involving serious damage or injury. Existing damage to your car should be reported when you enter Romania. If you are stopped by the police, stay in the driver's seat with your hands on the wheel.

The police can issue tickets on-the-spot, which can be paid at post offices; for serious offences, the police have the authority to immobilise vehicles. There have been cases of credit card fraud, so it's recommended to pay for fuel in cash.

SPEED LIMITS (km/h)

Towns/villages	50	
Main roads	90 / 100 (80 / 90 new drivers' first year)	
M'ways	130 (110 new drivers)	

GENERAL RULES

Drink-drive limit	0.0
Children in front seats	Min 12 yo and 1.5m height, even with restraint
Min driving age	18 (24 to hire car, with licence for at least two years)
Licence or IDP	✓ UK photocard or three-part pink licence required; other EU and US/CAN/AUS/NZ licences accepted for up to 90 days
Insurance: Green Card	✓ Recommended
DRL	○ Required outside built-up areas; dipped headlights preferred
Mobile phones	⊘ Handheld phones prohibited / ✕ Hands-free tolerated, but not recommended
Radar detectors	⊘ Prohibited
GPS speed camera alerts (POI)	✕ Not recommended (law evolving)
Emergency services	112

Special rules
- Priority to the right: give way to vehicles approaching from the right (unless signs indicate otherwise)
- Traffic on roundabout has priority (unless signs indicate otherwise)
- On two-way streets, park facing direction of traffic

i romaniatourism.com/travel-advisory.html#drivingromania

DRIVING EQUIPMENT

⚠	Warning triangle	○	Two required
🦺	High-vis jacket(s)	○	Required for all passengers
🧰	First-aid kit	○	Required
🧯	Fire extinguisher	○	Required for cars registered in country; recommended for visitors
💡	Spare bulbs	✓	Recommended
⛽	Spare fuel (can)	✓	Allowed (max 10L), must be empty when leaving
⚙	Winter tyres	○	Winter tyres mandatory on snowy/icy roads 1 Nov-31 Mar
❄	Snow chains		

TOLLS

🛣 Road tax to use all roads	
	Electronic vignette ('Rovinieta') available for seven/30/90 days or one year
How to pay	Buy at border, from post offices and filling stations or online
i	www.roviniete.ro/en/
🚗	Some bridge crossings over Danube

Russia

Videos of horrifying accidents in Russia abound online, and driving here is not for the faint-hearted! Avoid driving at night if at all possible. A road modernisation programme is under way, but outside the main cities, roads are frequently in poor condition. Many signs are in Cyrillic script only, so a satnav could prove helpful.

Although not compulsory, an International Certificate for Motor Vehicles (ICMV) and a Carnet de Passage en Douane may simplify border formalities, especially if you have a high-value car.

The police carry out regular spot checks and can issue fines, which should be paid through local banks. Many filling stations only accept cash, and there is limited availability of LPG. Diesel can be of variable quality: stick to the major chains if you can.

SPEED LIMITS		km/h
Towns/villages	(60) / (20)	residential zones
Main roads	(90) / (70)	new drivers' first two years
Motorways	(100) to (110)	as signed

GENERAL RULES	
Drink-drive limit (g/l blood)	0.0
Children in front seats	Min 12 yo, unless suitable restraint used
Min driving age	18 (22-25 to hire)
Licence or IDP	○ IDP required
Insurance: Green Card	○ Required (must specify Russia), or take out local insurance at border
DRL	○ Required outside built-up areas; dipped headlights preferred
Mobile phones	⊘ Handheld phones prohibited ✖ Hands-free tolerated, but not recommended
Radar detectors	⊘ Prohibited
GPS speed camera alerts (POI)	✔ Allowed
Emergency services	112
Special rules	

- In towns, forbidden to turn left other than at junctions with traffic lights
- Use of horn prohibited in built-up areas
- Forbidden to pick up hitch-hikers
- Offence to drive dirty car
- Call police to all accidents

Police checkpoint

Stop

Car wash

Restriction applies on Sat/Sun/holidays

DRIVING EQUIPMENT		
Warning triangle	○	Required
High-vis jacket(s)	✔	Recommended
First-aid kit	○	Required
Fire extinguisher	○	Required
Spare bulbs	○	Required
Spare fuel (can)	⚠	Import prohibited, allowed in country
Winter tyres Snow chains	✔	Winter tyres recommended
Additional items	✔	Recommended: ICMV and Carnet de Passage en Douane Recommended: inventory of caravan/trailer contents

TOLLS	
Road tax to use all roads	
How to pay	Pay at border

136

Serbia

I f you plan on visiting Belgrade, Serbia's capital, by car, there are three colour-coded parking zones: Red (one hour), Yellow (two hours) and Green (three hours). Outside the city, extensive roadworks can cause delays. When overtaking, local drivers often sound their horn to warn they are coming through, and may expect you to use the hard shoulder to get past. You should keep your indicator on throughout any overtake.

Speed limits vary widely, so watch for signs. Signposts can be in either Latin or Cyrillic script, so a phrasebook and satnav may both come in handy. The police can issue on-the-spot fines, which should be settled at a bank or post office within eight days. As in many countries in the region, existing damage to your car should be recorded when you enter Serbia. If you have an accident while in the country, complete a European Accident Statement form (see page 15) and have any damage certified by the police.

LPG ('Plin') is widely available; modern diesel-engined cars should use 'Eurodiesel.'

SPEED LIMITS — km/h

🏘 Towns/villages	(50) / (30)	near schools
🛣 Main roads	(80) / (100)	dual carriageways
🛣 Motorways	(120)	

GENERAL RULES

🍸	Drink-drive limit (g/l blood)	0.3; 0.0 for new drivers (first year)
🧍	Children in front seats	Min 12 yo, even with restraint
♨	Min driving age	18
❋	Licence or IDP	✅ IDP recommended
🪪	Insurance: Green Card	Recommended, or take out local insurance at border (check with insurer)
⚙	DRL	⭕ Required; dipped headlights preferred
📱	Mobile phones	⊘ Handheld phones prohibited
		⊗ Hands-free tolerated, but not recommended
📡	Radar detectors	⊘ Prohibited
📷	GPS speed camera alerts (POI)	✅ Allowed
🆘	Emergency services	112
⚓	Special rules	

- Priority to the right: give way to vehicles approaching from the right (unless signs indicate otherwise)
- Traffic on roundabout has priority (unless signs indicate otherwise)
- Do not overtake school buses at stop
- Horn may not be used in built-up areas or at night, except in immediate danger
- New drivers (first year) may not drive 2300-0500
- Visibly intoxicated passengers may not travel in front seat

i www.serbia.travel/useful-info/arrival/car

DRIVING EQUIPMENT

⚠	Warning triangle	⭕ Required (inside car), two if towing
🦺	High-vis jacket(s)	⭕ Required (inside car) for all passengers
🧰	First-aid kit	⭕ Required
🧯	Fire extinguisher	✅ Recommended
💡	Spare bulbs	✅ Recommended
⛽	Spare fuel (can)	✅ Allowed (max 5L, duty payable
⚙	Winter tyres	Winter tyres (min 4mm tread depth) or snow chains, mandatory on driven wheels 1 Nov-1 Apr
❄	Snow chains	⭕
🧳	Additional items	⭕ Spare wheel or repair kit Tow rope (min 3m) Nationality sticker (even with Euro-style number plate)

TOLLS

🛣	Tolls on motorways
💳	How to pay — Cash/credit cards/tag

i www.putevi-srbije.rs

Slovakia

There's plenty of good news to reassure foreign motorists planning a trip to Bratislava or the beautiful Tatra mountains: roads in Slovakia are generally in good condition, and there has been a big improvement in accident rates in recent years. Driving in Slovakia is relatively straightforward, but note the special speed limit of 30km/h for 30m before all level crossings, and clear your car of all snow and ice before starting off in winter. Local drivers sound their horns in case of danger, but also when intending to overtake. Credit cards are usually accepted at filling stations, and LPG ('Autogas') is readily available.

Border crossings on some minor roads are restricted to local traffic. At main frontier posts there have been reports of petty criminals who may damage your tyres and later try to charge you to repair them. Police officers can issue – and collect – fines on-the-spot, but may use their discretion to reduce the amount payable if there are mitigating circumstances. If you have an accident which causes damage to any property, you must report this to the owner.

SPEED LIMITS
km/h

Towns/villages	(50)	
Main roads	(90)	
Motorways	(130) / (90)	in urban areas

GENERAL RULES

Drink-drive limit (g/l blood)	0.0
Children in front seats	Min 12 yo, 1.5m height and 36kg, even with restraint
Min driving age	18 (21 with licence held for at least one year to hire car)
Licence or IDP	✓ UK photocard or three-part pink licence recommended
Insurance: Green Card	✓ Recommended
DRL	○ Required; dipped headlights preferred
Mobile phones	✓ Handheld phones prohibited ✗ Hands-free tolerated, but not recommended
Radar detectors	⊘ Prohibited
GPS speed camera alerts (POI)	✓ Allowed
Emergency services	112
Special rules	• Vehicles entering roundabout have priority • Give way to trams and buses • GPS devices must not be mounted in middle of windscreen
i	slovakia.travel/en/car-transport

DRIVING EQUIPMENT

Warning triangle	○ Required (inside car)
High-vis jacket(s)	○ Required (inside car) for all passengers
First-aid kit	○ Required
Fire extinguisher	✓ Recommended
Spare bulbs	○ Required (except for xenon, neon & LED bulbs)
Spare fuel (can)	✓ Allowed (max 10L)
Winter tyres / Snow chains	○ Winter tyres (min 3mm tread depth) mandatory on all wheels 1 Nov- 31 Mar, or beyond if conditions dictate
Additional items	○ Spare wheel or repair kit and wheel wrench Tow rope Nationality sticker (even with Euro-style number plate) Recommended: inventory of caravan/trailer contents

TOLLS

Tolls on motorways	
How to pay	Vignette (sticker) Available for ten days/one month/one year Buy at frontier, post offices and filling stations

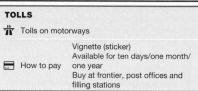

138

Slovenia

f you've driven in Germany, many of the rules in Slovenia will already be familiar. When joining a main road, vehicles should merge in turn. If traffic backs up on the motorway, leave space between the lines of cars so that the emergency services can get through. Even if you're in no hurry, it's worth buying a temporary motorway vignette, as road closures sometimes entail diversions onto the motorway network.

In cities, as with 'yellow box' junctions in the UK, you should not enter a junction unless your exit is clear. More unusual is the requirement to use your hazard warning lights when reversing. Fines for traffic offences are high, but are reduced if paid within eight days.

SPEED LIMITS   km/h

🏠 Towns/villages	(50) ((10) / (30) in some areas)
🛣 Main roads	(90) / (110) dual carriageways
🛣 M'ways	(130)

GENERAL RULES

🍷 Drink-drive limit (g/l blood)	0.5; 0.0 for new drivers (under 21 and first two years)
🧒 Children in front seats	Min 12 yo and 1.5m height, unless suitable restraint used
👥 Min driving age	18 (21 with licence for at least two years to hire car)
✳ Licence or IDP	✅ UK photocard or three-part pink licence required; IDP required for non-EU licences
🪪 Insurance: Green Card	✅ Recommended
☀ DRL	⭕ Required; dipped headlights preferred
📱 Mobile phones	⊘ Handheld phones prohibited / ❌ Hands-free tolerated, but not recommended
📶 Radar detectors	⊘ Prohibited
📷 GPS speed camera alerts (POI)	✅ Allowed
➕ Emergency services	112
🔧 Special rules	

- Priority to the right: give way to vehicles approaching from the right (unless signs indicate otherwise)
- Traffic on roundabout has priority
- Forbidden to use horn at night or in built-up areas, except in immediate danger
- No parking within 3m of pedestrian crossings

i www.slovenia.info/en/Getting-around.htm?kako_potovati=0&lng=2 and www.promet.si (traffic info)

The annual motorway vignette (Vinjeta)

Pass, showing height & number of bend

DRIVING EQUIPMENT

🔺 Warning triangle	⭕ Required (two if towing)
🦺 High-vis jacket(s)	⭕ Required (inside car) for all passengers
🧰 First-aid kit	✅ Recommended
🧯 Fire extinguisher	⭕ Required
💡 Spare bulbs	⭕ Required (except for xenon, neon & LED bulbs)
⛽ Spare fuel (can)	⚠ Import prohibited, allowed in country (max 10L)
⚙ Winter tyres	⭕ Winter tyres (min 3mm tread depth) or snow chains, mandatory on all wheels 15 Nov-15 Mar (beyond if conditions dictate)
❄ Snow chains	Approved snow socks accepted as alternative to chains

TOLLS

🛣 Tolls on motorways	
💳 How to pay	Vinjeta/vignette (sticker) available for one week/one month/one year Covers car & trailer Buy at border or filling stations
i	www.dars.si
🔘 Other tolls	Karawanken Tunnel (A2)

Ukraine

Since 2014, the political situation in Ukraine has been highly unstable, and foreign visitors are recommended not to enter Crimea and other areas. Check with the authorities in your home country before you travel; for UK citizens, see the Foreign & Commonwealth Office website at www.gov.uk/foreign-travel-advice.

If you're bringing your car to Ukraine, a translation of your vehicle registration document – in the form of an International Certificate for Motor Vehicles (ICMV) – will be helpful.

Although the country's main roads are generally in good condition, driving is hazardous, especially at night, with many accidents. Road signs – including those for speed limits – are inadequate or ignored, and many local drivers drive too fast and fail to signal when turning. If you undertake a long road trip, take some spare fuel in a can and sufficient cash to fill up. Accusations of corruption in the traffic police were rife until recently, but the authorities are working hard to improve this situation. If you do receive a ticket from the police, fines should be paid at a bank within 15 days.

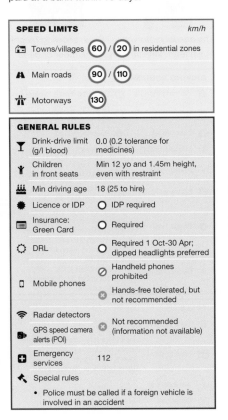

SPEED LIMITS *km/h*

Towns/villages	**60** / **20**	in residential zones
Main roads	**90** / **110**	
Motorways	**130**	

GENERAL RULES

Drink-drive limit (g/l blood)	0.0 (0.2 tolerance for medicines)	
Children in front seats	Min 12 yo and 1.45m height, even with restraint	
Min driving age	18 (25 to hire)	
Licence or IDP	○ IDP required	
Insurance: Green Card	○ Required	
DRL	○ Required 1 Oct-30 Apr; dipped headlights preferred	
Mobile phones	⊘ Handheld phones prohibited	
	✗ Hands-free tolerated, but not recommended	
Radar detectors		
GPS speed camera alerts (POI)	✗ Not recommended (information not available)	
Emergency services	112	
Special rules	• Police must be called if a foreign vehicle is involved in an accident	

Toll (cash)

No parking zone

Dip in road

Restriction applies on workdays

DRIVING EQUIPMENT

Warning triangle	○	Required
High-vis jacket(s)	○	Required for all passengers
First-aid kit	○	Required
Fire extinguisher	○	Required
Spare bulbs	○	Recommended
Spare fuel (can)	✓	Allowed
Winter tyres	○	Winter tyres (min 6mm tread depth) mandatory in snowy/ice conditions Nov-Apr
Snow chains	○	Use as signed
Additional items	✓	ICMV recommended

TOLLS

Free

Ukraine

Further information

Throughout this guide, you will find links and QR codes taking you to websites which provide fuller information than can be included here. To help you prepare for your trip, and maybe refresh your driving skills before a long trip, the following books may be useful:

Books

The Essential Driver's Handbook, Bruce Grant-Braham (Veloce Publishing, 2013)

How to be a Better Driver: Advanced Driving – the Essential Guide, John Sootheran (Institute of Advanced Motorists, 2009)

Roadcraft: The Police Driver's Handbook (Police Foundation, 2013)

If you plan on driving extensively in one country, it may be worth downloading or buying the local equivalent of *The Highway Code*: these include the *Code de la route* (France) and *Reglamento general de circulación* (Spain).

Staying current

For fast changing information, such as the latest fuel prices or traffic conditions, websites and social media are the perfect complement to the information in this guide. Below is a selection which you may find helpful, along with QR codes to scan to take you directly to the relevant website:

Real-time traffic information
www.viamichelin.co.uk

... and on Twitter @DriveEurope

Drive Guide Guru
www.driveguide.guru/europe

Fuel prices
www.fuel-prices-europe.info

Motorway and national road tolls
www.tolltickets.com

Mountain pass opening dates (dependent on weather)
www.oeamtc.at/portal/berg-passstrassen+2500++500408
(in German; 'Sperre' means closed)

City centre access regulations and charges
urbanaccessregulations.eu

Security advice (for UK citizens)
www.gov.uk/foreign-travel-advice

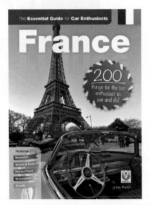

Index